WHEN
GOD
Smiles

Understanding the Heart of God
in Painful Circumstances

ERNEST J. COWPER-SMITH

DESTINY IMAGE EUROPE™ srl
Via Maiella, 1
66020 San Giovanni Teatino (Ch) - Italy
"Changing the world, one book at a time."

This book and all other Destiny Image Europe™ books are available at Christian bookstores and distributors worldwide.

To order products, or for any other correspondence, please contact:

DESTINY IMAGE EUROPE™ srl
Via Acquacorrente, 6
65123 - Pescara - Italy
Tel. +39 085 4716623 - Fax: +39 085 9431270
E-mail: info@eurodestinyimage.com

Or reach us on the Internet: **www.eurodestinyimage.com**

ISBN: 978-88-89127-56-8

For Worldwide Distribution, Printed in Italy.
1 2 3 4 5 6 7 8 9 / 12 11 10 09 08

Dedication

I would like to dedicate this book to all pastors who have been put on the back burner of ministry because of the failure of a marriage or something equally as devastating. May you find the grace to live your dreams again and a place that will accept you as you do.

Acknowledgments

I want to express a heartfelt "Thank you, Dear!" to my wife, Lyn, who has encouraged me to never give up on this project. She has believed in me when I've hardly believed in myself. Lyn, you're the treasure at the end of my rainbow!

To my pastor, Gary Carter, who is truly an apostle with a father's heart. You've made leaders out of boys and fathers out of men. You've taught me to never give up, because failure is part of the learning process on the road to success. God bless you in your mission to see God's Kingdom come into the hearts of all Canadians and peoples around the world.

To my children who have endured through all the dark days and uncertain nights while I've learned my life lessons. You have taught me how to forgive, that love truly conquers all, and that there really is a silver lining on the other side of the storms of life. You have always been there to love unconditionally and forgive quickly; and my heart continually swells with love and pride. May the experiences and the struggles we have faced together bring great eternal and earthly rewards to both of you!

To Rita Moir and Brad Belva, thank you for your labor of love during the "Listening Prayer Ministry," and for helping me to discover the deep hurts, and finding healing and deliverance. It changed my life forever!

Endorsement

I heartily recommend *When God Smiles* as a testament to the fact that tough times brings us closer to God and the resources we would have never gotten to any other way. If you are going through a difficult situation, allow Ernest Cowper-Smith to encourage you with the comfort that he has been comforted with. The truth, as this book so powerfully expresses, is that God uses messes to make miracles. Problems are the building blocks of miracles. If you need strength or encouragement, this book has hope!

Dr. Ed Delph
President, Nationstrategy
Author, *Making Sense of Apostolic Ministry*,
Church @ Community, and
Learning How To Trust...Again

Table of Contents

Foreword

The concepts presented in this personal journey of pain and discovery are a testimony of one man's life experiences; but as I was reading, I found myself reflecting on my own journey as well. Each chapter of this challenging and inspirational book has triggered a self-analysis and has caused me to reflect on who I am and how I came to be what I am today.

One of the most provoking thoughts in *When God Smiles* is the teaching on the revealing of one's inner nests, which caused me to stop and consider how many of my reactions and ways are really not responses to the present circumstances but a release of something just below the surface of my character.

I have considered outbursts of wrath, joy, love, rejection, and pain and have realized that many of my responses are overreactions due to past inner nests of pain and experiences. Although I have been successful in life, rejection continues to trigger a personal and deep pain, and I often need approval. In the past I have learned to work through these situations and overcome their effects, but by reading this book, I have now been challenged to deal with the root of this pain.

I also appreciate that this book isn't simply a testimony about emotion or about a journey, but is a Bible-based instruction manual of inspiration, guidance, and encouragement.

In John chapter 8, Jesus teaches that we shouldn't see things from the narrowness of our experiences. The Bible also says that as a man thinks in his heart, so is he. *When God Smiles* has challenged me to renew my thinking, deal with the inner nests of pain, and search for a greater future. This book has helped me to realize that even while God intends good things for us and we can usually avoid many unpleasant circumstances, we still become blinded by work, vision, business, or just plain apathy and miss the warning signs we often so easily see after it's too late. Consequently, I am taking another look for the warning signs of troubles in my life.

Indeed, we can be at the center of God's will and purpose for our lives and still be hindered by past experiences and inner pains. This thought has inspired me to reevaluate my own ministry. We might be doing what the Lord has called us to do and even attain a level of measurable success, but still, we must ask ourselves the following questions: Are there areas where I am being held back? Can I improve in any way? Do I need to deal with some past issues in order to go on to greater blessings? Personally, I don't have all the solutions yet, but this book has inspired me to press on and discover the answers.

While this book cautions the reader with warnings, at the same time, it brings hope as we learn how God has always been at work in Ernie's life and family. I know these things firsthand because I was there. His transparent testimony shows the depth of the work the Lord has done in his life. His accounts are accurate, and the victory is true. And it has been a great privilege to be a part of Ernie's life as well as that of his family's. I have been particularly challenged by the testimony of Ernie's marriage and am convicted not to take anything for granted or to presume that people will always be there and circumstances will always be the same. Consequently, I am now determined to be more aware and appreciative of my health, my ministry, my family, and my marriage.

This book is an expression of a man after God's own heart. The good news for us all is that the final chapters have not yet been written. We all can make changes, deal with inner pain, and look forward to a better tomorrow. As Ernie says, "The outward blessings are a reflection of inward change." As we apply the principles in this book, may we live out our lives and leave our unfinished legacy for future generations to follow.

Pastor Gary Carter
Drayton Valley Word of Life Church,
Drayton Valley, Alberta, Canada.

Introduction

For in the end, the things that matter most are not really things, after all.[1]

Phil Callaway

My goal is to introduce to you the powerful principles and promises from God's Word that have recently affected a great change in my life. By reading and learning these truths, you too can walk in the fullness of life that God has intended His creation to enjoy from the beginning.

For almost 40 years, I have been serving God with a deep conviction that He has saved me, cares for me, and is concerned about the everyday things that happen in my life. I know my sins are covered by the atoning work of Christ; my future in Heaven is secured by the victory over sin and death at the cross and His resurrection; and there is healing provided in the stripes that Christ bore for me. Indeed, I have personally experienced powerful healing touches on several occasions. I know my spirit is saved, and eternity and death hold no fear for me. I believe that my soul is being transformed as I "work out my salvation with fear and trembling" (see Phil. 2:12). And yet, it was only a few years ago that I realized that I had not been really experiencing the "fullness of salvation" and all of God's blessing in my life.

The truth is that while knowing and believing the promises and principles of salvation, I was still being held captive to and influenced negatively by events from my childhood that had left deep scars in my soul. Hidden memories that were locked away deep within my subconscious were triggering inordinate responses to everyday interaction with innocent people. These unseen pockets of poison hidden in me would, given the right stimuli, erupt and spill out deep feelings of rejection, guilt, fear, or anger, which were seldom a direct or appropriate response to what was happening in my life at that moment. They were like buried or hidden rocks and stones in the soil of my life that, as time passed by, were being pushed ever closer to the surface of my psyche by the frost of the winter seasons that life inevitably brings. After each eruption, there were periods of relief and peace until the inner poison built up enough pressure in me to erupt once again. It became an endless cycle that continued like a merry-go-round until my life spun out of control, leaving me heartsick and staggering from the loss of family, home, and many friends.

I've come to realize that although we are Christians, it is still possible for us to become trapped in a cycle of struggles and testing followed by defeat. Ultimately, these cycles of defeat hinder us in fulfilling God's divine plan and purpose for our lives. In this book, I wish to address commonly asked questions that have plagued many of us, including: What is at the root of these cyclical failures? Why do we have to start over at square one, struggling to learn what God is trying to teach us, and invariably face the same challenges, only to fall to the enemy's traps and snares all over again? Have you ever wondered why some people bounce from church to church struggling to find a church home and are always getting hurt by someone's actions or words?

Perhaps there are others who have experienced a cycle of failed marriages, lost jobs, anger issues, abuse issues, or broken friendships. They face the same issues over and over, only to lose the battle time and time again. These cycles of struggle and failure are the devices the enemy of our souls uses to prevent us from walking into the destiny and purpose that God has created for us. Ultimately, they hinder and sabotage us, as we as members of the Body of Christ work to fulfill the greater purposes for the Church on this earth. It is the enemy's way of keeping us, as soldiers of the army of God, out of the battle. And yet, we have been given authority to defeat his forces and win victory over his kingdom of darkness.

My sincere hope is that you will come to understand why it is that in some of our Christian homes, marriages, workplaces, and ministries, the enemy has been able to successfully strip us, rob from us, and even take lives. We'll also appreciate why Paul warned us in First Corinthians 11:24-34, that members of the Body of Christ can suffer unnecessary sickness or even a premature "sleep" (death), when they do not honor and recognize how vital it is to keep their relationships with each other free of unforgiveness, judgment, envy, and strife.

In the summer of 1995, I was deeply affected as I read Max Lucado's book, *He Still Moves Stones*. One particular chapter entitled, "The Sack of Stones," was actually the catalyst that began a process of healing and change that is still in progress today. Through the subsequent journey, I was urged by the Holy Spirit to journal my experience and the lessons God was teaching me. Hence, you will find that my earliest attempts to put my story on to paper are in their original form. This book has been a process of fits and starts, writing and rewriting, as was the experience of learning and relearning, proving and disproving many things that formed my worldview and distorted God's truth in my life. Entries in the first chapter of this book are dated as to when I wrote them, as are other excerpts in this book, taken from my journal, according to when I experienced them or put my thoughts and prayers on paper. When sharing the details involving my first wife, our friends, and the breakdown of our marriage, I have chosen not to use their real names in order to protect their privacy.

Even though I have gone through various storms and years of heartache that have written the divorce chapter of my life, I especially want you to understand the importance of God's best design for a marriage of lifelong commitment. For various reasons, both within my own soul and that of my first wife, our marriage failed. But it is not God's will that any marriage should fail, any more than anyone should perish eternally. Marriage is the pattern on this earth of the relationship that we as Christ's Bride are to have with Him. Yet because of our earthly weaknesses, God's grace has been spread wide to cover our failure to keep the bonds of matrimony intact. For where sin abounds, grace much more abounds. However, God's abundance is not licence to sin.

From the records of my prayers, life events, and conversations with God, and His subsequent work in my life, springs forth this account of God's awesome miraculous power, endless love, bountiful grace, and constant faithfulness. My deepest desire in writing this book is to bring hope and help to those of you who are in the midst of pain and suffering, and to help young Christians early in your walk so you do not become discouraged or surprised at the trials and tribulations you will experience as you mature. I pray that it will bless you and that you too will discover the transforming power of God in your life, which will prosper your soul so that you might walk in the fullness of His blessings every day of your life, and even experience the "Job restoration" of "more than twice as much."

ENDNOTE

1. Phil Callaway, *Making Life Rich Without Any Money* (Eugene, OR: Harvest House Publishers, 1998) 25.

CHAPTER I

The Storm Looms on My Horizon

How does one tell a story without an end? Well, at least not the end you might be anticipating as I begin the tale! I expect that by the time this book goes to print, it will be complete. Whether it bears the ending anticipated or something equally as triumphant I will know only as the days ahead unfold. And if the story has no ending yet, then where does one begin the telling? I will start somewhere in the middle. One thing I can say I've learned is that you can't live the tomorrows before they arrive, and no amount of rehearsing can change the way you've lived the past. So all that's left is to live one day at a time, breath by breath, step by step, walking in it as God directs your path. To tell this story requires several trips into my past, and as painful as it is, it affords the effort all the same. So...here goes...

JANUARY 22, 1999

It is an exceptionally beautiful January night in 1999. The snow is falling softly and silently. I pause, quietly staring up at the street lights and watch the grand flakes drifting down. They melt on my face as they mingle with silent tears. I have this overwhelming sense that it's not only the snow that's falling down around me. My whole life in a few moments of revelation has shifted its course and is tumbling senselessly around me as well. As if I'm in a dream or a spectator watching a movie, I hear my wife's laughter as she teases and throws snowballs at a friend who we've invited to live with us for the past few months.

In winters past, my wife and I had taken many walks in the snow together, and it was always such a special time for us. On nights like tonight the air was warmly romantic as we walked hand in hand, tossed snowballs at each other, or playfully shoved each other into the snowbanks. But tonight it is different. It is as if I am invisible, and she is alone with him.

As I look at the two of them, having fallen down into the fresh snow ahead of me, the truth of what I am witnessing hits me like a blast of cold air in the middle of a January storm, stealing my breath and chilling me through to the bone. I am not prepared for it, but in retrospect, the signs have been there for some time now. Funny how a man can refuse to see what he doesn't want to see even if it has been staring him in the face for a while. Blindness is more than a product of infatuation; it's also the result of stubborn pride.

I force my body to move ahead and follow them back to the house. Shock has settled in, and I will myself to move through the motions of stripping off winter clothes and then retire to our room to try to absorb the revelation.

Steve has gone to his room, and Cindy (my wife) has slipped into the bathroom to run a hot bath. Amidst a whirlwind of emotions and terrifying thoughts tumbling around in my mind, I somehow bring myself to face her to confront my fears. After gently knocking and hearing the door unlock when I announce who it is, I step into the washroom. I ask her quickly lest I lose the nerve, "Cindy, when did you stop loving me?" She looks up with surprise. I think hearing these words coming from me is a shock, for I never have been one to admit that she might not love me or might ever think of leaving me. In fact, even the word divorce has not been allowed in my vocabulary, let alone considered as a threat to our marriage.

[*I did not believe in divorce then, and to even entertain the thought was paramount to committing a terrible sin. I recall in the heat of a terrible disagreement shortly after we were married 19 years before, I tried to forbid her to ever entertain the idea of divorce, separation, or speak of leaving me again. It was a big mistake. It put up bars around her and created a sense of being trapped. And you can't feel security or love when you're trapped. As I learned later, there had been many times that I had reinforced that invisible barrier, which only added to her sense of bondage. And now this caged and frightened bird was about to attempt to break out of her seemingly inescapable cage.*]

There is a brief silence as the words hang in the air and are swallowed by the rush of bathwater tumbling from the tap into the tub. Then with a quiet sigh and very little hesitation or emotion, like a person who has inwardly hoped to be caught and is tired of the long charade, she replies, "About two years ago." She glances at me to see if the arrows are hitting their mark.

Well, they cleanly score, and the inescapable truth finally sinks in. It is a triumph of sorts for her, I suppose—not that she wants to hurt me. For in the past three or four years, during the seasons of rough marital waters, on several occasions, she has tried to verbalize her feelings; yet never quite being able to say it outright or convince me to really listen, she finally dropped the topic. Now I am admitting openly as reality that which she has never been able to get me to believe was possible before. Half the battle is won—telling me is one thing, but getting me to believe it is quite another. [*And as she will discover in the many months ahead, my accepting it as final will be a totally different matter.*]

OCTOBER 22, 2002

Writing these words alone in my apartment almost four years after that pivotal snowy day in January of 1999, I realize that I still believe there is a love in her buried deeply beneath the hopelessness and pain of all the broken dreams that brought us to this place. It might be enough love to rebuild our marriage on, should we both accept the healing and forgiving power of Christ. My prayer is to restore in her enough hope that she might yet have her dreams and needs fulfilled while being my wife. But only time will tell how the pages of my life will unfold or what will be written on them. How one year or even one month in time can change your picture and vision of the future has been proven to me several times over in the past few years.

OCTOBER 2002–FEBRUARY 2004

[*I did not write during this period, as I concentrated on establishing a new life in another community. Meanwhile, I met my new wife, developed a career in social work, and built a new home. Much of what I share about my inner healing and restoration took place during this period.*]

FEBRUARY 5, 2004

I have always felt that somehow the God I served from my youth would come and rescue me. I also felt He had directed me to write about my journey; and from the painful experience of separation, the loss of my dreams, and eventual divorce, I would minister to others. Several months after my first wife and I were separated, I sensed Him showing me that a book would come out of the experience, and it would minister to other hurting people. I can recall reading or hearing somewhere that "hurting people hurt people." I realized that as I reviewed the words I had written in the first part of this chapter, I was still hurting deeply. Perhaps that is why I laid the proverbial pen down and couldn't put to paper the things that my Lord had been teaching me through it all until I had experienced several months of intensive inner healing.

CHAPTER 2

Why the Furnace, Lord? Why?

I have refined you but not in the way silver is refined. Rather, I have refined you in the furnace of suffering. I will rescue you for My sake—yes, for My own sake! That way, the pagan nations will not be able to claim that their gods have conquered Me. I will not let them have My glory! (Isaiah 48:10-11)

GOD SMILES

When our eyes are opened and we truly see
The designs of God for you and for me,
Then without a fear or a doubting thought,
We'll truly embrace the trials we've got.

The crushing of grapes brings forth the wine;
Through bruising the rose, it's perfume we find.

The Refiner's fire makes the metal so strong,
Its value increased while the Master works on.

Why run from the press or the fire escape
If when He is through…God smiles.

Ernest Cowper-Smith
September 1999

Thank God, there is a Chapter 2. Aren't you glad there can be new chapters to our lives? Maybe you've just written or are in the process of writing some very painful or seemingly purposeless chapters in your life. Perhaps you've seen your dreams, hopes, possessions, friends, or loved ones disappear from your world. And maybe just maybe, you've been holding on to the hope that your life will be filled with happier days and meaning; yet year after year has passed you by, and the happier chapters of life have not materialized. In fact, each time a chapter is written, it just gets worse. Can I ask you, friend, not to put down this book until you've read the end account of the latest chapters that God has written in my life. Like Job of the ancients and many others who have endured the fire, I can look back and without regret say, "Look at what God has done!"

It has been several years since the world I lived in came apart on that snow-filled winter's day in January 1999. The landscape of my life has changed so dramatically that sometimes I feel like I'm living in another dimension completely. I realize that after the work God has done in my life, He truly is the Master Potter who can take the broken and shattered people who lay around His feet, paralyzed by their own sins and ignorance, and put all those pieces back together. Then after enveloping them in His awesome love, He gently drops them as a softened lump of clay back on His "wilderness wheel" of providence and tribulation. Next, He lovingly molds that precious life into an awesome work of art, another masterpiece, with His stamp of authority and approval on it. And nothing, my friend, is as valuable as a masterpiece by the greatest Artisan of all time!

A CHILD'S FAITH

I was just a child when I first knew that my life was in the hands of a loving God who cared deeply for me. My memories of my younger years are sketchy at best, but I can recall scenes or little vignettes of my life as early as three and four years old. I had great faith as a child, which was evidenced by the miracles and answers to prayer I would see even as a preschooler.

Sometime during my fourth year in this world, our beloved kitty-cat was hit by a car. Several hours later, it was discovered on the highway out in front of our home. My mom told me years later that its cold and lifeless body had been brought in to the porch to await a burial out behind the house. However, when I was told about our loss, I refused to accept it and insisted that we should pray for my kitty. (I think I must have gotten the idea from watching Mom and Dad pray for us daily and from the vacation Bible school I had attended that summer.)

I was not to be dissuaded from my determination to pray for the cat; so shortly thereafter, my mom accompanied me to the back porch where I apparently laid hands on the cat and told it to live, just as the story from the Bible had been related to me. And it immediately recovered. Its bones were knit together, its inner wounds were healed, breath returned to its lifeless body, and it got up onto its feet. We enjoyed that cat for many years to come as God honored the faith of a little four year old and raised a stone-dead cat from his grave.

REFINED BY FIRE

Can I tell you, my friend, that God is still raising the "dead-cat" marriages and lives that have been hit by the enemy's "semi-trucks" on the highways of this life? He is still the God of the resurrection, restoration, reformation, and second chances, if we'll submit to Him and listen to His warnings. The Lord longs to return all that the enemy has stolen from His children, but unfortunately, we get impatient because we've been conditioned to be an "instant everything" generation. However, God's solutions and answers to the predicaments we get ourselves into don't come in a "Minute Life" box. "Get a perfect life in just five minutes" is not advertising you'll find anywhere in His Word.

I've come to realize that there is no magic formula or secret process that will turn your life into a bed of roses overnight. In fact, if you truly dig into the Word, you find quite the opposite. God never intended for His children to have a carefree life of leisure and ease, although He does know how to create a life that is so filled with the fragrance of His love and grace that you and others feel like you're standing in a bed of roses. He truly wants His children to lead a triumphant and joy-filled life. And for this to happen, there is a process, which is no secret. It comes with flags waving, horns blaring, lights flashing...and a price tag—He promises tribulation, persecutions, difficulties, storms, and battles. The Book of John guarantees it! *"...In the world you will have tribulation..."* (John 16:33 NKJV). And it would seem as you read the life accounts of the disciples in Acts, that the more mature you become in your faith, the more challenging the obstacles you will face. Life becomes one great adventure after another. Are you up for a great adventure? Then read on, good heart, read on!

In this chapter, I deal with the principle of the fiery furnace. There is a purpose to everything that comes into our lives. If you find this difficult to accept, then at least acknowledge the fact that God is so powerful that He can turn any evil event into a perfect opportunity to display His glory and power and bring good from what satan has intended for evil. Suffering and tribulation have never been favorite subjects of mine. For many years, I felt that once you became a Christian, suffering would be eliminated by God from your life. But it is now clear that all pain and suffering in life comes as a result of choices. Some heartache and pain are a result of our own choices, some from other people's choices, and ultimately all from the choice that Adam and Eve made to disobey God.

It is not that God gains some kind of perverse enjoyment watching His creation go through suffering and pain. Rather, when given the choice between a season of pain and tribulation that helps us, or a life of ease and leisure that eventually leaves us weak and useless to His Kingdom, we would always be wise to accept the former. God is always there to turn our trials into triumph, pain into patience, and sorrow into serenity. Later in this book, I will go into more detail concerning my own personal Job experience and the lessons we can learn from the Book of Job; but for the moment, let's look briefly at Job 36:13-16, which paints a vivid picture of the way two different hearts can respond to suffering and how it changes the outcome.

> *The godless in heart harbor resentment* [against people and God]; *even when He fetters them, they do not cry for help.* [The result:] *They die in their youth, among male prostitutes of the shrines.* **But** those [righteous who don't rebel] *who suffer He delivers in their suffering;* **He speaks to them in their affliction.** *He is wooing you from the jaws of distress to a spacious place free from restriction* [inner freedom], *to the comfort of your table laden with choice food* (Job 36:13-16 NIV).

This has been my own experience. The Lord gave me this Scripture as my promise on August 26 and again on September 1, 2002 before I moved to Drayton Valley, Alberta, and experienced the intensive healing process that followed my move there. I literally felt the release from the jaws of distress, from

31

resentment, and from fear and insecurity; and then I found freedom to love again. The following years I experienced the twofold blessings as His promises came true in my life, just as it did for Job. The fire process is always worth it in the end.

❧❧❧

GOD IS ALWAYS THERE TO TURN
TRIALS INTO TRIUMPH,
PAIN INTO PATIENCE,
AND SORROW INTO SERENITY.

❧❧❧

EXPERIENCING THE GREATNESS OF GOD'S GLORY

John proclaimed that Jesus the Messiah would come after him and said, *"He will baptize you with the Holy Spirit and with fire"* (Luke 3:16b NIV). In Acts chapters 1 and 2, we see this fulfilled not only literally when they witnessed tongues of fire descend on them as they were filled with the Spirit, but also metaphorically throughout the rest of the Book. We find that the comfortable lives of many of the believers were totally turned upside down with persecution and death. God allowed this outcome at the hands of Saul and many others in order that they would be driven out of their comfortable place in Jerusalem and could turn the rest of the world right-side up with the Gospel! One man or woman's time of trial and difficulty became another man's opportunity to hear the Good News! First Peter 4:12-13 also prepares us for and encourages us through these times of difficulty.

> Dear friends, do not be surprised at the painful trial [KJV says, "fiery trial"] you are suffering, as though something strange were happening to you. But rejoice that you participate in the sufferings of Christ,

32

*so that you may be overjoyed **when His glory is revealed*** (1 Peter 4:12-13 NIV).

Also, in Isaiah 48:10-11, the prophet Isaiah says:

*I have refined you but not in the way silver is refined. Rather, I have refined you in the furnace of suffering. I will rescue you for My sake—yes, for My own sake! That way, the pagan nations will not be able to claim that their gods have conquered Me. **I will not let them have My glory!*** (Isaiah 48:10-11)

God gives us another special promise that is of great value to our eternal well-being:

*In the world **you will have tribulation;** but be of good cheer, I have overcome the world* (John 16:33b NKJV).

Because John assures us we can expect "tribulation" and First Peter 4:12-13 assures us that no fiery trial or test is meant to surprise us or take us unaware and to be overjoyed when His glory is revealed, then I would think that we are being set up to experience the revelation of some further *glory* of God that we previously have not seen! Somehow in someway, God intends for us to act in faith rather than in fear, and in such a manner that His power can be released in such a magnificent way that great glory is given to Him. Subsequently, His blessing can be released to us.

What is the term, "glory of God," referring to? We don't often use the word *glory* today, except in reference to the accolades we give to a superstar of sports or perhaps a great war hero. But it's much more than that which we bestow on others. In this context, it's a reference to all the awesome power that God possesses. It's the totality of His divine character wrapped up in the triune Godhead and the unbounded perfection of His creation revealed in all things we know and see in this universe. It's the uniqueness of His relationship to us as His children, spiritual beings created in this finite earth yet for an eternal fellowship that glorifies Him. It's all of this; and yet considering every discovery and everything we have learned in all fields of science, considering every thought, word, song, picture, or form of expression with which we have attempted or conceived to convey God's wonders, we have glimpsed and proclaimed only the equivalent of one grain of sand among this world's entire supply of sand.

His glory is what scientists have recently discovered holds this universe together. We used to say that space was a vacuum, empty between all the incredibly powerful stars that store immense amounts of energy. But recently I learned from a DVD series on the Book of Genesis by Dr. Chuck Missler[1] that world renown physicists have discovered there is more power and energy packed into one square centimeter of empty space than in 100 million suns integrated over 100 million years. They now know it is this energy, also called zero-point energy, that prevents the electrons, which are flying around neutrons, from escaping and flying off into space. They are held in place by this zero-point energy.

In reference to Christ, the Book of Colossians says,

> *Who is the image of the invisible God, the firstborn of every creature: for by Him were all things created, that are in heaven, and that are in earth, visible and invisible, whether they be thrones, or dominions, or principalities, or powers: all things were created by Him, and for Him: and He is before all things, and by Him all things consist* (Colossians 1:15-17 KJV).

This term *consist* in Greek is *sunistao*, from which the word *sustain* is derived; and it literally means "held together."

Even though the world of science wants to refer to this energy or invisible force as zero-point energy, we know that it is

Christ Himself in the expressed glory of God who holds this universe together, electrons to neutrons, which balances the planets around their suns, the stars in their constellations and galaxies where He placed them at creation. In addition, we know that we are to house, to radiate, to reveal and be a conduit, if you will, for that glory to be shown to this corrupted world through the person of Jesus Christ, which He also declares in Hebrews *"**The Son is the radiance of God's glory** and the exact representation of His being, **sustaining all things by His powerful word**"* (Heb. 1:3 NIV). He further expounds on this to say,

> *In bringing many sons* [us] *to* [or into, or to share in this] *glory, it was fitting that God, **for whom and through whom everything exists**, should make the author of their salvation perfect* [complete] ***through suffering*** (Hebrews 2:10 NIV).

Even thousands of years before this, King David was inspired to declare: *"The heavens declare the glory of God; and the firmament* [this term, raqia, can correctly be rendered space or aether—the substance of space] *sheweth* [reveals] *His handiwork"* (Ps. 19:1 KJV).

His *glory* has substance, permanence, completeness, and light—light meaning an extradimensional source of revelation and existence. It's revelation, knowledge, wisdom, and power, working together to create and sustain the realm God dwells in, and in which we may also coexist. It's not a substance or material that can be erased, eliminated, altered, or cancelled out. It's the absence of nothing and the substance of everything. It's also the complete revelation of the Father as we see it in His Son, Christ Jesus, as He commanded the demons and spirits to do His bidding, controlled the waters of the seas that He walked on, stilled the storms and raging elements around Him, created limbs where there were none, returned breath and life to rotting corpses, and restored sight to the blind and health to the sick.

*Father, I want these whom You've given Me to be with Me, so **they can see My glory. You gave Me the glory** because you loved Me even before the world began!* (John 17:24)

When we look at the life of Christ, His works, His teaching, His love, kindness, faithfulness, and His complete character, we see God's glory being revealed to man, the culmination of it being revealed on the cross and in His resurrection! *Glory* is so much more than praise and recognition coming from man to God. It's God reaching down to become vulnerable as He puts His whole preeminence in the hands of man. So, the glory of God will do far more to change not only the world around us but to change the world within us. God wants to give it to us, but He will not entrust that glory to just anyone of this world. It is far, far too much power to place in the hands of the unrighteous who would use it for selfish purposes. Ultimately, it could be used to destroy God's work rather than to reveal God's heart! Jesus longed for the day to come when He would see the glory of God not only resting for a moment of time on man, but taking up residence, dwelling in, influencing, motivating, and empowering men, women, and children of every race and age.

I have given them the glory You gave Me, so that they may be one, as We are—I in them and You in Me, all being perfected into one. Then the world will know that You sent Me and will understand that You love them as much as You love Me (John 17:22-23).

GOD'S GLORY REVEALS THE GOOD AND EXPOSES THE EVIL

I'm convinced that as God's glory rests on us or in us, it attracts the good things of life to our world. As the good gathers in our lives, the negative, the evil, the corrupt will be exposed. Light and darkness cannot dwell together. Einstein said, "Light always expels darkness as darkness is simply the absence of light." God wants to unearth in us anything that hinders the fullness or the complete wonders of His glory from being seen in our lives, so that they can be seen just as they were seen in the life of His first Son, Jesus Christ. When the things that are buried begin to surface, they bring with them a set of rules or a system of consequences.

For example, when you take a stick and hit an old hollow tree that contains a wasps nest, you will activate a programmed response within each of the wasps that will result in an attack on you. Even though you might not have seen the nest of wasps, they were still there all along. The wasps weren't troubling you much at first, but those little suckers have a way of multiplying and becoming annoying when you're trying to enjoy a picnic or barbeque on a warm summer's day. Then they get disturbed by some little inadvertent incident and, "wham!" you discover quickly that the nest is there! Consequently, you find yourself in a situation where you need to make a choice to either deal with it properly—get rid of it, or try to keep ignoring them until you can't ignore them any longer. This usually happens when some-one ends up in anaphylactic shock!

God in His infinite wisdom allows us to experience the circumstances so that these hidden nests can be revealed in our lives before they hurt us and others, and so that His glory can be revealed to others through our response to these situa-tions. The Bible calls these occasions, "fiery trials." I think the best biblical example of this principle of fiery trials and how it functions to change us or our circumstances is the story of Paul and Silas preaching in Philippi, the capital city of Macedonia (see Acts 16:16-38).

Paul and Silas were stripped naked, beaten mercilessly with many stripes, and then cast into a dark, damp, urine and feces-laden, rat-ridden prison cell in the deepest, coldest part of the prison. These details are significant because they reveal how afraid the owners of a fortune-telling slave girl were of Paul and Silas' message to the public, and how seriously they wanted to punish these men who had taken their source of livelihood by setting the young woman free from a spirit of divination. And to add insult to injury, not only were they beaten and cast into the filthiest part of the prison to die of infection and starvation, but their feet were also fastened in stocks (shackles with chains). How much worse of a scenario can you imagine? How much more of a hopeless situation for escape can you think of? And still, they went one step further by posting a security guard at the door and charging him with his life if these men were to escape!

But God saw this as an opportunity to display *His glory*; and in order for Him to do so, these men of God needed to respond appropriately in this situation. They needed to exhibit the right attitude, remain positive, and look at the situation from a heavenly "God is still on the throne" perspective. We can see plainly from First Peter 4:12-13 and Isaiah 48:10-11 that God allows the painful trials to refine us and present an opportunity for Him to be glorified. His glory will always be revealed in those dark and hopeless times when deliverance comes!

But how much more glory will we display as we turn our hearts to Him in adoration and trust. As we trust Him with our lives and choose to adopt an attitude of faith while looking at the bright side of things, we not only attract others to us but dispel the evil influences from our presence. Satan's forces can't handle being in the presence of God's children when they're full of the Spirit and overflowing with praise to God. As we focus on worshipping Him, He will respond by flooding our hearts with peace that surpasses human understanding and logic. It's not logical to be happy and full of joy, full of song, or to hold on to a positive attitude. I'm sure that some of the prisoners who were Paul and Silas' cellmates thought the two of them had "flipped their lids." But the secret to overcoming is the attitude we choose to take while in the dark and desperate situations. We must always be ready to give God glory and praise in spite of our circumstance.

And the story tells us in Acts chapter 16 that they in their pain and degradation did just that. In the most disgusting, horrible, and painful circumstances, they began to sing songs of praise and love for their God who counted them worthy to suffer for Him. They prayed, and they believed that God was in control. They didn't let *circum-stance* dictate their *faith-stance*. Instead, they stood on the promises, worshipped their Creator and the One in control of the situation, and prepared for whatever God had in store that would bring more glory to Him.

They were waiting...no, they were more than waiting...they were preparing for God to act. It was not a passive "woe is me," preparing for the worst. It was not even a bite-your-tongue, don't-complain, just-endure-this, kind of preparing. Rather, it was an active, faith-engaged, turn-your-eyes-toward-Heaven-in-praise-and-expectation, kind of preparing! And when it came, it came in a big, earth-shattering way—an earthquake shook the entire prison, setting everyone free. Every prison door was opened; every shackle and chain fell off!

And the result for the prisoners? Many were added to the Kingdom of God! And while the prisoners remained where they had been chained, Paul and Silas called out to stop the jailor from taking his own life. Consequently, he fell at their feet in repentance, gave his heart to Christ, took Paul and Silas home to clean their wounds, and clothed them. Then in the middle of the night, he awoke his entire household so that Paul and Silas could preach the Good News of Christ to them. The Bible says that immediately after hearing his testimony and the Gospel, the rest of the family and his entire household turned over their lives to Christ.

GOD IS ALWAYS IN CONTROL

And that's not the end of the story. God did something to the hearts of the magistrates so that they changed their minds as to how to handle Paul and Silas. They sent word with their sergeants to the jailor that these men were to be released. Little did they know these men were not even under their authority and control! How do you release that which you don't have under your authority? And that's the thing—Paul and Silas *knew* whose authority they were under. They knew who was really in control. And so, the truth was that while they were in circumstances that suggested they might spend their lives in a pretty bad situation, they knew that the reality was totally different than the natural conditions that appeared to be in control of them. And that is the secret to being able to turn every difficulty or every obstacle into opportunity—every messy thing into a blessing thing! Recognize whose authority you are under and who really controls your circumstance and situation; and when things get to looking pretty grim, start by looking up to Him and pray for God's peace to come. Speak to the storm that rages inside your mind. Say to it, "Peace! Be still!" Then praise Him for your opportunity to bring glory to Him again!

This is one of the principles that kept me from giving up on my life and my future when I had lost my family through separation and divorce. Every day I would listen to worship music. Every day I would thank God for my friends and family who were praying for us. I didn't praise God for the separation or when I learned of the impending divorce, but I did praise Him for who He is! I knew that in spite of our humanness that brought about the circumstance I was in, He was ultimately in control and could turn any evil thing into blessings and victory, and work it out for my good. On Sundays, I would lose myself in worship and write down the messages that my pastor preached. I wrote down the thoughts that God would give me and looked for God's heart to be revealed. I listened for His voice to speak to my heart and give me a new hope.

For two years while He taught me patience and endurance, I desperately looked for where God was leading me. And one day He did speak to me! He directed me to not lose hope and that His promises to me would come. He put a light at the end of the dark tunnel I was stumbling through. I kept getting up, going to work, pinching pennies to pay the bills while supporting my children, and helping my wife make the house payments. It seemed to be without purpose, and I strongly identified with the character Tom Hanks played in the movie, *Sleepless in Seattle*. When he talks on the phone to a talk show host, she asks him how he has been coping since losing his wife. He says something to the effect that he just breathes in and then out, breathes in and then out, living one day at a time. And that's what you do while re-minding yourself every day that God still loves you. He still loves your spouse or ex-spouse, as the case might be, and He is still weaving together a fresh hope and a glorious future for you.

David Martyn Lloyd-Jones wrote a book in 1965 entitled, *Spiritual Depression, Its Causes and Cure*. In his chapter on "Faith", he quotes this wonderful line: "Behind a frowning providence you find a smiling face." He goes on to say:

Now hold on to that. You say that you do not see His smile. I agree that these earthborn clouds prevent my seeing Him, but He is there and He will never allow anything finally harmful to take place. Nothing can happen to you but what He allows, I do not care what it may be, some great disappointment, perhaps, or it may be an illness, it may be a tragedy of some sort, I do not know what it is, but you can be certain of this, that God permits that thing to happen to you because it is ultimately for your good. *"Now no chastening [correction] for the present seemeth to be joyous, but grievous; nevertheless afterward it yieldeth the peaceable fruit of righteousness"* (Hebrews 12:11).[2]

So what's your story? What's your situation? What difficulties, impossible circumstances, or chains are keeping you burdened down with cares? What dark and damp prison walls seem to be closing in on you? Don't look at the natural situation; don't focus on your own needs, feelings, or pain! Don't dwell on the negative aspects of life, but rather look toward your Creator and praise Him, because in reality you're on the verge of an exciting opportunity to not only witness God's glory revealed to you and all around you in similar circumstances, but to participate in expanding the Kingdom of God and His righteousness in your life as well as others. Isn't that exciting! Doesn't that make life an adventure worth living for rather than drudgery worth leaving! Watch for the *"greater glory of God"* (see 1 Pet. 4:12-13) to be revealed in the *"peaceable fruit of righteousness"* that springs forth (see Heb. 12:11 NKJV) from the manure that's been cast onto the soil of your life.

GOD'S LOVE AND GLORY
SHINE THROUGH THE FURNACE

Paul especially had a life marked with hardships after turning his life over to Christ. Read Second Corinthians 11:16–12:12, and notice the list of things he endured—shipwrecks; damp, rank prison cells; beatings; humiliation; unjust arrests and court cases; hunger; and desertions. And we get the distinct warning that learning to expect some difficulties is a wise way to prepare for the Christian walk. (This is especially applicable for those who have a call to the ministry as apostles.) Difficulties, tribulations, trials, hardships, inner struggles, and pain are signs that God is working in our hearts and our lives to perfect His child until he or she reflects the glory of God through them. He is simply preparing us and causing us to grow in our faith and salvation. The good news is that this furnace process brings us closer and closer to a state in our inner man where nothing can shake our faith in God. It implants a peace that is beyond human comprehension and it becomes so much a part of our souls that those around us not only see it in us but can draw strength and encouragement for themselves from it. The furnace process burns up more of us, our old carnal nature, so that more and more of Him, His Holy Spirit in us, might shine through.

Let me explain how this furnace process works in our lives. Usually, we begin this transitional process that starts when we are unredeemed souls full of selfish ambitions and desires. In this state, we are not displaying true godly character. God's divine love, His glory, or His presence do not shine through us. We might display good works, love for mankind, or godly character qualities, but the source of these is still our own human character; and our motives might vary from self-righteous pleasure or selfish desires that cause us to control and manipulate others for our own purposes, or an inordinate striving to receive man's or God's recognition, acceptance, or praise. These all boil down to self-idolatry! In many cases, we are trying to earn God's approval and attain a place in Heaven through our own works.

You're cruising through life thinking all is well when "bam!" one day God hits you with the truth revealing your true inner heart to you. We hear the true Gospel, the price God paid for us already by purchasing our salvation on the cross. We believe and respond to it in faith. We cease our striving to earn eternal life, and we turn our hearts and lives over to Him and find ourselves being changed. Our likes and pleasures change, our motivations change, our hopes and dreams change, even the things we dislike change as we're given a new character. Sometimes these changes happen slowly in certain areas of our character, sometimes quickly in other areas, but changing nonetheless to a place where others notice a distinct difference in the way we respond to how life treats us. They see God's love and glory shining through us even when things are falling apart around us, and they want that thing which we have that sets us apart. It becomes evident that the worse the situation becomes, the more powerfully God's love is seen in us. This transformation and refining process continues to where more and more of God's love and glory is seen in us on a daily basis, regardless of how good or bad life appears to be for us. We become a powerful light in the darkest place and hour of the night. Then how quickly we are able to draw others to Christ as we contrast against the backdrop of an evil generation!

ENDNOTES

1. Dr. Chuck Missler, *The Book of Genesis, An Expositional Commentary, DVD Series* (Coeur d'Alene, ID: Koinonia House) disc 1, session 3.

2. David Martyn Lloyd-Jones, *Spiritual Depression, Its Causes and Cure* (London: Lowe & Brydone Printers Ltd., 1965, reprinted in 1972), 145.

CHAPTER 3

Pushing up Daisies or Pushing up Stones

For if you live according to the sinful nature, you will die; but if by the Spirit you put to death the misdeeds of the body, you will live, because those who are led by the Spirit of God are sons of God (Romans 8:13-14 NIV).

And they that are Christ's have crucified the flesh with the affections and lusts (Galatians 5:24 KJV).

In the same way, count yourselves dead to sin but alive to God in Christ Jesus (Romans 6:11 NIV).

"Pushing up daisies"—I don't know where the expression came from or how long ago I first heard it, but I know it is used to make inference to someone who has passed away and has been buried in the traditional way. Flowers, or daisies, as has often been the case, are planted on the fresh grave site. Hence, the terminology, "pushing up daisies," has come to mean that someone is physically dead to this world and in their grave. In like manner, when we have died to self and have surrendered our lives to Christ, another process begins, which I call "pushing up stones."

WORKING OUT YOUR OWN SALVATION

As we walk this new life we have in Christ, we learn how to put our own nature with its fleshly lusts, desires, and selfish motives to death. We learn how to die daily. And as we die to self each day, we find we're not "pushing up daisies" as the saying goes, but "pushing up stones" (and sometimes big rocks) that have been hindering the seeds and promises of God's Word from flourishing in our lives. Each year that passes reveals another fresh pile of stones for us to deal with, but fortunately, they become fewer and fewer while the harvest in our lives grows more bountiful. (We'll study this process more in-depth in Chapter 6.) This experience is the essence of the "fiery trial process" and the "dying to self" experience. Every year that goes by should mean we are closer to the place where we become completely transparent; there is little of our old selfish nature left in control, and more of the Spirit of God and His character shines through. Ultimately in eternity, only the glory and nature of God will be seen in us.

The following verses reveal that the growth process is a very evident part of our belonging to the family of God.

> *Therefore if any man be in Christ, he is a new creature: old things* ***are*** *passed away; behold, all things* ***are*** *become new* (2 Corinthians 5:17 KJV).

Note that the tense of the verb in this verse is singular present. It says, "...*old things* ***are*** *passed away; all things* ***are*** *become new*"—not *have*, not will, but ***are***. Thus, we are in a constant state of tension or change. It is an ongoing process that has no end. The reason it cannot end is because although we are not "of this world," we are still a part of it. We have our feet in the world's dirt and are daily soiled by contact with our own earthly lusts, desires, and pleasures that are fed by this world. So the process must be continual. Let's look at another verse and again you can see that the wording chosen also indicates a process:

> *You must be even more careful to put into action God's saving work in your lives, obeying God with deep reverence and fear. For **God is working** in you, **giving you the desire to obey Him and the power to do** what pleases Him* (Philippians 2:12b-13).

The New Century Version (NCV) reads:

> *Keep on working to complete your salvation with fear and trembling, because God is working in you to **help you want to do and be able to do** what pleases Him.*

There is often a distinct desire in us to please God, yet the power to do the right thing evades us. I remember seeing a plaque on the wall of a fellow student's apartment in Bible school some 28 years ago; its message is still relevant today: *"If it pleases you to please God, then go ahead and please yourself!"* I like that! If you really think about it, it makes perfect sense. Nothing should please us more than making God happy with our growth as His children. And in order to do so, our motives and desires must be changed if we are to be successful in living out our salvation by faith.

Our salvation is "worked out" (see Phil. 2:12b NIV, NKJV). Does this mean we *work for* our salvation? Not at all! If it said, "working for," that would mean you were in the process of trying to earn something you did not yet have. *Working out* applies to something you already have.

For example, the Word says, *"The **wages of sin** is death..."* (Rom. 6:23a NIV). Before we confess our sin and turn to Christ for salvation, we've already been put on the payroll in satan's army; and whether we realize it or not, we're *working out* our rewards with Him. Our wages have already been guaranteed; it just becomes a matter of how terrible they will be. We're already earning and reaping the wages of sin. Even Christians are reaping the results of sin on earth. Every nation that is at war is reaping the wages of sin; every family who has a relative battling cancer is reaping the wages of sin. Every nation dealing with the Asian Bird Flu, AIDS, colds, leprosy, or any other disease is also dealing with the wages of sin. All death, hatred, sin, and sickness began first with Adam and Eve; subsequently, everyone today is impacted. When the unjust suffer from sin, the consequences can also be experienced by the just.

However, there is an escape from the ultimate outcome for the unjust—"*...but the gift of God is eternal life*" (Rom. 6:23a NIV). Aren't you glad for those big "*buts*" in the Bible! Salvation is *a gift* from God, which we receive by faith in Christ and through repentance and confession of our sin.

Let me explain it to you another way. The *working out* terminology is comparable to a person born with the gift of music hidden away within him, which is yet to be discovered and released. Everyone is eligible to receive the gift of salvation. God makes it clear that He wants all to be saved. Once we hear this Good News and respond by opening our hearts and lives to His reign and control, we are given the gift of eternal life. In that moment of reaching out by faith and believing the Good News, we receive the gift of eternal life. From this point on, we begin to participate in cooperation with God and the work of the Holy Spirit in us, of being refined and molded into the perfect image of His Son. We are *working out* our salvation, and it never stops until we are made complete in Heaven. The world's population can be divided into two groups and only two groups in respect to eternity. There are people who *have* received this gift and those who *need* to receive it in order to know peace and rest in their souls. Salvation is that place where our sole desire and pleasure is to *become the image of Christ on earth.*

REFLECTING GOD'S GLORY

I also believe there is an inner longing that is in our deepest spirit or subconscious to again *radiate His glory, which we were originally clothed with in the garden,* by being in His presence. Romans 8:23 puts it like this:

> *And even we Christians, although **we have the Holy Spirit within us as a foretaste of future glory**, also groan to be released from pain and suffering. We, too, wait anxiously for that day when God will give us our full rights as His children, including the new bodies He has promised us* (Romans 8:23).

It's that hidden desire within every human being to know the love and acceptance, the fellowship and presence of their Creator. When Moses came down from Mt. Sinai after spending time in the presence of God and receiving the Ten Commandments, the Bible says His face shone with the glory of God, although he wasn't even aware of it.

> *When Moses came down the mountain carrying the stone tablets inscribed with the terms of the covenant, he wasn't aware that his face glowed because he had spoken to the Lord face to face* (Exodus 34:29).

Verse 30 tells us that this glory was so bright that the people were afraid to approach him; he had to cover his face when he came out into public. Apparently, it did eventually fade; however, it remained substantial for some time. So because we have a daily invitation into God's presence (note: the veil in the temple that hid Moses and God's glory from the naked eye was torn in two at the cross) should we not, having taken advantage of this free access into God's presence, also begin to reflect God's glory? And if this glory, which was visible to the witnesses of Moses descent from God's presence on Mt. Sinai, is also the same glory that Paul calls the Holy Spirit, then it's reasonable to expect that there might be times, after we have been in God's presence in prayer or worship, corporately or privately, for prolonged periods, when a certain glow becomes visible on our faces to the natural eye also. In all probability, you will not even be aware of it when it occurs! I'm not saying this will happen or should happen; rather, we should not to be shocked or afraid if it does happen.

"I WANT THAT GLOW TOO!"

I can think of at least two examples in my life when the glory of God was shown. Once when I was 15 years old, I went with my father to a Friday evening of praise and prayer at friend's place out in the country. It was six months after I had been baptized in the Holy Spirit, and I was hungry for all God had for me. During this prayer meeting, I was battling with thoughts, memories, and distractions of every sort, which the enemy was throwing my way to keep me from really entering in to God's presence in my spirit, and I was rebuking these thoughts quietly. At previous prayer meetings, I had sensed God's presence so powerfully, and the gifts of the Spirit had flowed through me and others freely; but this evening in my spirit, I could not enter in or find relief from my carnal nature or the enemy. Finally at nearly 11 o'clock, my friend Bob and I said good-bye to everyone, including my father with whom I had come. I remained there to spend the night and then to work for Bob on the farm the next day.

While Bob chatted with my father outside as he saw him off, I stood in the lane 50 yards from the house. Most of the house lights had been turned off as well as the bright yard light. I turned my eyes up to the night sky and was absolutely blown away by the brilliance and number of stars I could see. (If you've lived in the city or town all your life, you might have never had the opportunity to witness such a sight. I encourage you to take a long drive late some night and get as high up and as far away from any ambient light as you can. Then you will understand what happened next.)

As I stood in total awe and wonder, an intense sense of the magnitude and beauty of our galaxy and God's hand of creation overwhelmed me. I became keenly aware of how small and insignificant man is, in the light of all God's splendor. I marvelled that while God is so powerful, He still chooses to come and fellowship with us. In my spirit, I sent up to my heavenly Father my deepest praise and worship for what He had given me. Just as quickly as this intense feeling of awe had settled into my heart, a deep sense of God's presence enveloped me. All I could do was lift my hands and quietly adore my Creator as tears streamed down my face! I stood there for at least 10 or 15 minutes before I turned and began to walk back to the house. As I turned to go back inside, I was oblivious to Bob who was also walking back to the house. As he caught up to me, he spoke; and when I turned around, I heard him gasp! "Ernie," he exclaimed, "you are glowing, I mean, literally, positively, glowing! What has happened out here?"

I struggled to put into words that which I was experiencing. I related my sense of awe and wonder at the night sky and God's beauty, and as I did, I received a word of knowledge for him—if he wanted the baptism of the Holy Spirit with the evidence of tongues, he could receive it right now.

You should know that Bob often worshipped in the Spirit in English with spontaneous lyrics and music that were beautiful. I knew in my spirit that he had an anointing on him, yet for some reason, he had never spoken in tongues, even though he wanted to.

We went inside, and I prayed a simple prayer while putting my hand on his forehead. He stood quietly shaking under the power of the anointing that I felt flowing through my hands into him. I saw him standing there as a clear vessel in the shape of a human being; and there was a liquid (the Holy Spirit) flowing through me which was filling this clear vessel. When the liquid reached his throat, he began to tremble even more; yet the liquid could not go above his vocal cords. In my spirit, I asked the Lord what the problem was and why he was having such difficulty. Instantly, God showed me the problem was a spirit of fear, which had shut his vocal cords to the heavenly languages that would normally come forth. I rebuked the spirit that had attached itself and told it to let go and leave. The very second I spoke the last word, Bob burst forth with the most beautiful and intricate language of praise. That night, which stretched on into the wee hours of the morning, was one of the most enlightening and incredible baptisms I have ever witnessed.

Several hours later after a short night of sleep, he came to wake me to help milk the cows. He told me that when he approached the room I was in, the presence of God was so powerful that he stood for some time outside the doorway. As he did, he became aware that I was praying in tongues. He waited before entering, thinking I was up; but finally, he opened the door to find me sound asleep yet praying while I slept. Later, he shared a memory that had come back to him the night before while I was praying for his baptism in the Holy Spirit. He said that as a boy of eight years old, he had an experience while rounding up their cattle. He too had stood on a hill not far away in awe of God's starry heavens and began to sing and yodel his praise to God. And like my experience that evening, he had felt the powerful anointing and presence of God settle on him. It was then he had broken out in several languages that he did not understand. Later, when relating the experience to his parents, he had been warned never to do it again or to tell others, because they thought it was demonic. It had placed a fear in him that had remained, even though he had completely forgotten the incident of his youth. Then when I rebuked the demon, the memory flooded back to him and along with it the freedom to worship in tongues and a fresh baptism in the Holy Spirit. This story is also evidence to the fact that forgotten incidents from our childhood can directly impact our lives today.

I also want to share the testimony of one young man whom my wife and I had been counselling. One Sunday evening, we invited Mark (not his real name) to join his brother, Jeff (also not his real name), and our worship team to play drums for our "Into His Presence" worship service. He had played the barroom scene with his brother's group many years before and was an accomplished musician like his brother on several instruments. He was not serving the Lord at the time, although he was really searching for more of God in his life. Normally, I wouldn't have invited a musician who wasn't serving the Lord to play on the team, but this time when his brother approached me about the idea, I felt strongly that it was a "God thing."

The evening was a totally new experience for him, and he sensed the presence of God in the place. He was quite amazed how the thrown-together band could instantly click together so well and how they seemed to just know where and when to play their individual parts as well as corporate parts. The music flowed from each of the members like a well-practiced orchestra. As he witnessed the divine leading and anointing of the Holy Spirit on us, He was awed by the reality of God's love, power, and the profound sense of peace he experienced while in worship. Later, he went home with a firm determination to find more of this God he had experienced and to let God guide his steps from then on.

Following the time of fellowship, he went to pick up his children at his neighbor's place. When the lady answered the door, she exclaimed, "Wow, you are glowing! Where were you tonight?

What happened? Because whatever it is, I want some of it too!" She was not a Christian; however, not only could she see the anointing's glow on his face, but she also felt the joy and love radiating from him! It attracted and drew her to God! Later, he would have opportunity to witness to her. The last I knew of her situation she had not yet turned her life over to Christ, but Mark went on to surrender his life to Christ. Now, he and his brother are serving the Lord with their gifts of music.

CLOTHED WITH HIS GLORY, OR NAKED AND ASHAMED

We can be clothed with His glory at all times to some degree or another. It might not always be visible, but I'm convinced that it should always cover us and be sensed by others. Moreover, it is protection from the enemy. When he attempts to find us, "we are hidden with Christ in God," "being clothed with power from on high"; hence, he cannot find any access to our lives (see Col. 3:3; Luke 24:49). This was the same state that Adam and Eve enjoyed—free access and full fellowship with the Father.

Genesis says, *"And they were both naked, the man and his wife, and were not ashamed"* (Gen. 2:25 KJV). But disobedience changed those circumstances.

> She took of the fruit thereof, and did eat, and gave also unto her husband with her; and he did eat. And the eyes of them both were opened, and they knew that they were naked; and they sewed fig leaves together, and made themselves aprons. And they heard the voice of the Lord God walking in the garden in the cool of the day: and Adam and his wife hid themselves from the presence of the Lord God amongst the trees of the garden. And the Lord God called unto Adam, and said unto him, Where art thou? And he said, I heard Thy

54

voice in the garden, and I was afraid, because I was naked; and I hid myself (Genesis 3:6b-10 KJV).

Before their disobedience, I believe that at the end of each day, they would stop their daily business of setting up house, harvesting food, and learning about all that surrounded them in the garden; and they would take time to walk through the garden with their Creator to learn from Him, to enjoy His company, and have an intimate time of fellowship. These times were not unlike what every young child should be able to look forward to when his or her loving father returns home from a hard day's work. I can envision that same anticipation and joy that children express as they climb up onto their daddy's lap to touch his face and be held in his strong arms. It's a safe, warm, carefree place of joy, laughter, healing, and rest.

Even so, Adam and Eve's daily load of cares and responsibilities were never more than they could bear. Their duties were never beyond their range of knowledge or expertise, and certainly never became so exhausting as to leave them sick or too physically tired to enjoy the time walking in the garden, exploring and learning about their wonderful and incredible world directly from their Father and Creator. To this day, every human's intuition or inner man is tuned to be able to hear God's voice beckoning them to Him as He searches their lives for that moment when they will respond, "Here I am, Father!" And it is only our shame and nakedness that causes us to run, hide, and try to clothe ourselves with self-righteous coverings of our own making, rather than run to Him and allow Him to receive us on His terms, washed clean of our shame by the blood of the Lamb of God, and covered in the righteousness of Jesus Christ. While we might be able to hide our true inner selves and all our sins and failures from one another with the facades we wear, we know, just as Adam and Eve knew, that the disobedience and sins we've committed are not hidden from the eyes of God. We've lost that wonderful covering of His glory and have been laid bare before Him.

Our daily lives are a continual string of opportunities and choices, which either bring God glory or diminish the glory that already rests on us once we've become His children. Everything we experience and every choice we make is really all about how we handle the shame of our nakedness and the inevitable exposure of our sinful, carnal nature before Him. Do we let Him clean us up, or do we attempt to cover it up and hide it?

ACCEPTING AND HARNESSING THE GIFT OF SALVATION

It is evident from several key terms that Jesus uses in the following passage that salvation is far more than the simple act of making our spirits alive unto Christ. It's the way we respond and deal with the trappings of life itself.

> Then Jesus said, "Come to Me, all of you who are weary and carry heavy burdens, and I will give you rest. Take My yoke upon you. Let Me teach you, because I am humble and gentle, and you will find rest for your souls. For My yoke is easy to bear, and the burden I give you is light" (Matthew 11:28-30).

In this Scripture, Jesus uses the term, "rest for your souls," which is a state of our mind, will, and emotions. "Let Me teach you" indicates a process to be learned from Christ through the Holy Spirit; and "my yoke is easy to bear" indicates by analogy a partnership (two oxen perfectly matched and pulling together under the bond of a well-fitted yoke) and cooperative effort by Christ and ourselves. We learn to release the control of our lives over to Christ, to cease from striving to steer our lives in the direction we think they should take, and allow the Holy Spirit to direct our daily paths. He becomes our strength, the fuel or the driving (motivation) force in us; and He uses our bodies as a host body (sounds sci-fi, I know, but the truth is in there nevertheless) to accomplish His will and purposes on this planet. But He can only do so if there has been a true desire and invitation for Him to enter our hearts and transform us from the inside out by the power of the blood He shed at the cross of Calvary for us.

This is the "free will" aspect of His human creation. I serve Him by choice, not by force or threat. I was not *abducted* into the Kingdom of God; I was *adopted* into His Kingdom. First, I was introduced and invited to join His family, and once I consented, I became an heir and joint heir with Christ to all that God has given over to His Son, Jesus Christ (see Rom. 8:14-17 NKJV). I share or identify not only with His suffering, but also in the glory that once rested on Adam and Eve before the fall. This glory hid them from their enemy and protected them when they were in the very presence of God the Father as He walked with them in the garden. There is a cost involved because we release control of our lives to Him, but our contribution or cost is so insignificant by comparison to His. He was willing to die for us so that we can live for Him and with His Spirit, the Holy Spirit, within us.

This relationship is rather like the elephant and the mouse that took a journey together. With the mouse on the elephant's back, they traveled together. One day they came to a chasm with a great rushing river deep below. The mouse was afraid of heights so he closed his eyes while they quickly crossed over on the swinging bridge, which was bouncing and swaying under their weight. Arriving safely on the other side, the mouse let out a great nervous sigh of relief and said to the elephant, "We sure shook that bridge, didn't we?"

Now, even though we're just along for the ride, so to speak, we must still be on board and participating in and cooperating with His work and plan for our lives. Personally, I'd rather be riding safely on the back of "the elephant" than crushed under His feet, for those who refuse His gift will ultimately receive His judgment. *"But all who reject Me and My message will be judged on the day of judgment by the truth I have spoken"* (John 12:48).

So even the people who do come to Christ for salvation must learn how to put on, to walk in (as you would a coat of armor), or to harness that gift, to work and cooperate with it until it flows out of their souls effortlessly. Let me be more specific by using an analogy of the gift of music within a concert violinist. It takes some discipline to become a virtuoso on the violin. And often those closest to the gifted person will put up with some very annoying attempts and painful practices, but that doesn't change the fact that the one blessed with the gift has been given a gift. We can see the improvement from month to month as they practice, and often we are amazed at how quickly they pick it up.

Now, if you've ever had to spend time with someone who has no gift from God as a violinist but has been striving to become one, you will understand why we call salvation a gift, even though for the gift to be evident we must "work it out." The person who strives to master an instrument, or who tries desperately to become a violinist but does not have the gift to do so will only destroy what would be truly appreciated by those who love music. They do more harm to our pleasure center for music than satisfying us. In fact, they can grate on our nerves and leave a very annoying feeling in us. They will do little to inspire or convince others to truly appreciate and desire to learn the instrument if that person has never seen or heard a true violinist before. Likewise, you might have met a few religious people who exhibit a self-righteous attitude and are striving to earn their way into God's Kingdom. Unfortunately, these religious folk have not discovered or received salvation as a gift from God, and they most undoubtedly will do more harm than good to the cause of Christ and His Kingdom.

Yes, salvation is a gift that involves a very real growing process in which God, supernaturally and in His divine wisdom, knows exactly what it will take to cause us to be stretched in our faith, increased in our patience, and deepened in our peace.

GOD USES PAIN TO DEVELOP A FAITH GAIN

We must remember that our faith is grown or expanded in the same way our physical muscles are built. When exercising and pushing our bodies beyond comfortable limits, we begin stretching and tearing the fibers our muscles are made up of. The body responds by repairing and filling in the gaps and tears of the fiber with more than was originally there. Bodybuilders know these facts and repeat a motto to encourage themselves to push their limits: "No pain, no gain!"

God has designed our spirits and souls the same way. The Father loves us dearly and will discipline us in many ways, using various means. We know by the difficulties and corrective measures He sends our way, that we are His children and that He dearly loves us. It's His way of preparing us to do great exploits and become exceptional warriors for His Kingdom.

> *I am the One who corrects and disciplines everyone I love. Be diligent and turn from your indifference* (Revelation 3:19).

> *Dear brothers and sisters, whenever trouble comes your way, let it be an opportunity for joy. For when your faith is tested, your endurance has a chance to grow. So let it grow, for when your endurance is fully developed, you will be strong in character and ready for anything* (James 1:2-4).

Thus, we are prepared to become an active member in the army that God has designed, so that we can combat the influence and work of satan on this earth, and to be *"ready for anything"* the enemy might throw at us in this life. Too many of God's children have become complacent and *indifferent* to the assaults of our enemy against those around us, and we fail to realize the great loss God feels when a sinner dies in his lost state. Are we letting the pursuit of pleasure and things or the cares of this world blind us and cause us to become indifferent to the task and privilege we have been equipped for—turning around the vast tide of humanity who are rushing to an eternity without God?

If we are to have developed a great faith that endures through anything that comes our way, we can expect a period of great pain to our inner man. Furthermore, like any growing child, when it comes to having strong bones and muscles, our diet is also critical for good health. Hence, Peter instructs us to long for, to desire with an intense desire, the things that will help us grow in our faith. Then as we mature, we are told we should be able to handle the meat of the Word, the truths that reveal the deeper elements of our faith. It is these deeper truths that are revealed through the painful trials and testing process.

In much the same way that a hot furnace brings the dross and useless slag to the surface to be removed when purifying gold or any other metal, likewise the Holy Spirit uses these periods of trial and pain to reveal the things we have hidden in our characters that are in conflict with God's wisdom and ways. We will always encounter difficulties and challenges to our moral and belief systems. Thus, it is important to be grounded in the Word, so that we find the truth that sets us free to walk in obedience to His will. It will always be an exercise of recognizing the choices before us; testing those choices through the grid work of the truth revealed to us; and then making and following the correct determination. It is not easy; it requires much practice and yielding to the voice of the Holy Spirit to make correct decisions consistently. We may stumble, favor wrong preferences, or get sidetracked from time to time; but we can always return to His faithful arms for comfort, strength, and acceptance. And He will always give us another opportunity to walk in His purposes rather than our own.

We all start with the basic principles of salvation to guide us, and then as we learn the deeper truths from God's Word, we grow up and succeed in becoming mature and strong enough to help others through the process.

> *You must crave pure spiritual milk so that you can* **grow into the fullness of your salvation** (1 Peter 2:2a).

But spiritual milk is only the first stage of this developmental process.

> *And a person who is living on milk isn't very far along in the Christian life and doesn't know much about doing what is right. Solid food is for those who are mature, who have* **trained themselves to recognize the difference between right and wrong and then do what is right** (Hebrews 5:13-14).

> *So let us stop going over the basics of Christianity again and again. Let us go on instead and become mature in our understanding* (Hebrews 6:1a).

> *Dear brothers and sisters, when I was with you I couldn't talk to you as I would to mature Christians. I had to talk as though you belonged to this world or as though you were infants in the Christian life. I* **had to feed you with milk and not with solid food, because you couldn't handle anything stronger. And you still aren't ready, for you are still controlled by your own sinful desires. You are jealous of one another and quarrel with each other.** *Doesn't that prove you are controlled by your own desires? You are acting like people who don't belong to the Lord* (1 Corinthians 3:1-3).

Within this Scripture is a simple test that reveals the stage where someone is at in their faith maturation process. Paul reveals that those who are *"still controlled your own by sinful desires"* are immature—an immaturity that is sometimes expressed by the desire to be identified with a single leader or spiritual hero. Could this mark of immaturity not also be seen by our tendency to want to exclude believers from Heaven, whose views are different from our own? Our own prejudices toward other denominations or Christian faith groups are, in my opinion, a sign of immaturity. They reveal a lack of understanding God's diverse nature, His design for the Church as a Body with many members, and His great grace and patience with us while we walk in ignorance. If we truly belong to the Lord, we'll love and accept our brothers in Christ! Very often we have only a small measure of grace and tolerance for those whom we perceive as being wrong in their beliefs. God will surely teach us just as any father would correct and discipline a child who is berating or mistreating a sibling. Because He loves us, He corrects us so that we will grow up; and His discipline can be painful.

THANKS FOR THE SPANK

I can attest to the value of teaching opportunities that come in large family settings. I grew up with six sisters and three brothers. Many times we endured the "board of education as it was applied to the seat of learning." I'll never forget the day my father caught me "cutting up" and "blowing raspberries" on my arm during family devotions. (Devotions were always called "prayer time." Mom or one of my older sisters would open the front door and at the top of their voice, so the entire neighborhood would hear and feel a deep conviction and repent, they shouted for us to come in. "Prayer time, you guys! Get in here now!" Seriously, they had to yell, because we all were scattered at various neighbors' homes, playing with our friends.)

On this particular Saturday morning, as I recall it, my older brother started it all with the "real thing." One of my sisters joined in, and I followed suit, of course. Now it's important to know that "prayer time" was a very sacred half hour in our home; yet to this day, we still share many funny stories and tales, implicating each other regarding this event. My dad turned from where he was kneeling, and in his deepened, "you're in big doo-doo" voice, told me to stick around when we were done, because he would be teaching me to respect the Lord's hour.

Well, I wasn't born yesterday, and I knew that he might forget, if prayer time were to drag on long enough. After all, Dad fathered the last of us when he was almost 60! So, of course, I prayed for a long time, and then I whispered to my sisters on each side of me to do the same. I'm sure Dad thought revival had finally come to his home on that Saturday morning as Mom and the others who "caught the fire" prayed at length. "And bless my auntie's big toe which she stubbed last week." Or maybe it was, "Bless all the starving kids in China, India, Bangladesh; and bless my sweet mommy and daddy—they're such wonderful parents." (A little buttering up would help right about now!) And so it went on and on. Needless to say, I scooted out of the house pretty quick 30 minutes later, thinking, *Surely he will have forgiven or forgotten by now.*

Prior to this Saturday morning's devotional time, I had hidden the swing seat, so I could "save the swing" from my sisters later and have it all for myself. Very spiritual kid I was! I had retrieved the swing seat and was just getting settled in to a real good "pump it up as high as I could go" time, when one of my sisters (likely the one who wanted the swing and ratted on me) came running out of the house and told me Dad wanted me in there "right NOW!"

Sure enough, he had the belt (a 2-inch wide by 14-inch long piece of combine strapping) in hand and was standing in the living room waiting for me. "You know what this is about, so hold out your hands!" he declared looking down on me with his best "I better make this serious" look. I held out both hands not knowing how many licks to expect; and then, the strap hit my right hand with one hard stinging blow. To this day, I do not know what came over me, but I looked up at him, smiled seriously, and said, "thank you!" He was so shocked and caught off guard that he began to chuckle. As he raised the strap again struggling to keep a straight face, his chuckle then burst into a laugh. And because the handing out of punishment was always a spectator sport in my home, the rest of the family also burst out laughing by this time as well. We all were laughing so hard that our father couldn't regain his composure or keep a straight face any longer. So, he gave up the idea of another lick and muttered, "Oh, get outta here!" I split without arguing, of course!

Now, when God disciplines us, we might not be able to laugh while in the middle of it, but I'm absolutely positive we'll be able to say a truly heartfelt "Thank you" to Him when we get to Heaven, hopefully sooner, if we seek wisdom and understanding here. The end results of His disciplinary actions are always good!

SEEKING HIS WILL AND
LISTENING TO HIS VOICE

God begins the growth process by sending situations our way that cause us to search His Word, to seek His will, to surrender to His Holy Spirit, and to draw strength from Him and encouragement from His Body (the Church family). But if we refuse to acknowledge that there might be a divine purpose to the painful trials and tribulations that come at us and to respond to them by asking for God's perspective and purpose for them, we might well be rejecting the very thing that we were praying for when we asked God to bless our lives, to use us for His honor and glory, or to heal our homes, marriages, or other relationships. We must always be ready to accept that we might be the one who needs to change in order for things to become better in our lives. We cannot blame our spouses, parents, churches, or anyone else for the situations we find ourselves in. All we can do is ask God, "Why has this happened to me, Lord? Have I allowed something to create a break in the hedge of protection that You have put around me? Is this situation coming as a result of my own doing, Lord, or do You have some divine purpose in it? What is it I am to learn from this trial You have allowed to come into my life? Show me quickly, Lord, so I can learn the lesson and get through this as soon as possible and be a stronger, more faithful warrior for it!"

GOD BEGINS THE GROWTH PROCESS BY SENDING
SITUATIONS OUR WAY THAT CAUSE US
TO SEARCH HIS WORD, TO SEEK HIS WILL,
TO SURRENDER TO HIS HOLY SPIRIT,
AND TO DRAW STRENGTH FROM HIM
AND ENCOURAGEMENT FROM HIS BODY.

How often has our ignorance and egos led us out into the highways of pride, rebellion, and unforgiveness, and consequently, our homes and children suffer the consequences? Perhaps we've failed to tune our spiritual ears into the quiet voice of the Holy Spirit. More often than not the real problem is that we've become dull of hearing because we have spent so much time entertaining ourselves with the world's distractions. Hence, our ears have lost the ability to hear the finer, subtle prompting voice of the Holy Spirit. We cannot listen to the din and pounding noise inside an iron works factory daily without ear protection and then expect to step into a lush forest and hear the symphony of beautiful and delicate sounds it holds.

The trees rustling in the breeze, water rippling in a brook, birds singing to each other, crickets and bullfrogs in the evening all joining together to create a profound experience, yet we would hear nothing except perhaps an occasional screech owl or coyote howling. Our spirits are the same; they become dull when bombarded every day with the noise of this world's pursuits and traffic jams. We absolutely must draw ourselves away from the rat race of life and find a quiet place to be alone with God and tune our spirits into His voice to hear whatever He desires to say to us on a daily basis. This daily process is where we draw our strength and hope to go on through every difficulty.

> *The Sovereign Lord, the Holy One of Israel, says, "Only in returning to Me and waiting for Me will you be saved. In quietness and confidence is your strength..."* (Isaiah 30:15).

Even while taking the time to listen and be alone with God, we can still consistently resist the Holy Spirit's gentle, quiet prodding and develop a blindness and deafness to the Holy Spirit's voice much the same way we develop a callous where the shoe rubs the foot or the hand wears against the shovel handle. Unfortunately, by this time, although He might be shouting at us to get our attention, we wander obliviously into the path of danger. The air horns might be blaring, our family and friends crying out their warnings, yet we continue to grope our way blindly and indifferently into the destructive situations of our own making. It takes a solid faith and trust to obey His voice, and discipline and determination to consistently draw ourselves away from this world and into the armchair of God's love. Here He welcomes us with outstretched arms to climb up onto His lap and let Him soothe away the bumps and bruises that this world has inflicted on us. It is in these places of quiet trust, inner healing, and listening to the soothing heartbeat of God where He reveals the areas which have become the hiding place for things that have hindered His perfect will for our lives from coming to pass.

Only as we develop our ability to hear His voice will we be able to go through life in this world and respond and obey even the little warnings He sends our way to protect us from the traps the devil would try to lay across our path. Let me close this chapter with this question: During the busiest part of your day, under the great pressures of responsibilities, deadlines, expectations, and crises, would you hear Him if He prompted you to pray or to share His Word? And if you did hear Him, would you obey?

CHAPTER 4

From Inner Injury to
Divine Intimacy

You have given me hope. My comfort in my suffering is this: Your promise preserves my life....It was good for me to be afflicted so that I might learn Your decrees (Psalm 119:49b-50,71 NIV).

God always has a purpose amidst the difficult situations we face, sometimes to grab our attention or to discipline us, other times to strengthen and mold us into His image, but always to glorify Himself in our lives. And no matter what the enemy might try to do to destroy us or our faith, God is able to turn that situation around and use it to bring glory to Himself and to serve His own purpose in our lives. When we truly get to the place where we trust His methods and accept His wisdom, we can embrace what life brings our way.

To help you understand just how this works, I want to share some of the more personal details of my journey through divorce as I struggled with the loss of ministry, income, home, friends, and the sense of direction and purpose in my life. Perhaps the most difficult aspect of my marriage breakdown was the loss of my identity. My whole life and identity had been wrapped up in who we were as a couple—parents, pastors, lovers, and friends. Having married young at 21 years of age, neither one of us had had the opportunity to truly discover who we were on our own.

In Cindy's case, she had moved from under her mom's roof directly to our home. She had been sincere in believing she would like to be a pastor's wife, but her underlying motive, I later realized, was not a ministry calling, but regaining a sense of security she had felt during her childhood and youth years when she was in the company of her pastor. She had grown up through most of her life without a loving and caring dad, and the only father figures she had known in her home had rejected and abandoned her and her mother. In addition, her stepfather had abused her and used her for sexual gratification. So, the trust, safety, and love she felt in the company of her pastor who took on the father figure role in her life, left her believing that life as a pastor's wife meant she would feel safe, secure, provided for, and loved.

Just as my wife had not truly discovered who she was on her own, nor had I. I had leaped into our marriage with the zeal of youth, believing that I had a firm grasp on my gifts and calling and that she was ready to follow me to the ends of the earth. I misjudged the power and strength of her family ties. In addition, my own pride and insecurities prevented me from seeing the deep issues buried in me that needed to be revealed by God's healing hand.

Being the middle child in a family of ten children had left a deep-rooted feeling of insignificance. All my life I had clamored for attention, to be heard and noticed. I was always getting into trouble for talking too much in school, and later for not knowing when to keep quiet while visiting at the table, in a restaurant, or a friend's home. The chastisement only served to reinforce my feelings of rejection and insignificance. There was always a struggle to be accepted among peers and to find a place where I fit in, to find something I was good at and felt valued for.

My childhood home life had a noticeable effect on the way I spoke and behaved after I grew up. Because our home was often loud and chaotic when I was a boy, I developed the habit of always speaking in a louder voice than was necessary to be heard in public settings. When I would get perturbed or the slightest bit upset, my voice would subconsciously get louder and louder to the point I was often told I was shouting at people, the children, or my wife without even realizing it. Even in the church choir or on the worship team, I would have to keep the mike from being positioned directly in front of me lest I drown out the quieter voices. I could often speak to larger crowds and not need a mike to be heard. These and other issues, which I will discuss in later chapters, were all hindrances to my finding a place where I belonged and discovering my true identity.

In spite of all these circumstances, I did my best to provide and balance the demands of ministry and family; yet the pressures of "living in a glass house" and continually trying to fix other people's problems, along with never having enough finances eventually took its toll on my wife and our relationship. She had to do something, and the options were few. She chose to get out of the ministry, separate, and eventually end the marriage. I made a decision to take a sabbatical from ministry for the sake of the health of our church and my own emotional health. Then, as I faced the possibility of a divorce and leaving the ministry, I struggled to find purpose and meaning in my life. The following excerpts from my journal reveal my desperation and how wonderfully God responded to teach me and help me through my season of floundering.

JANUARY 15, 2000

During my evening devotional time, I recorded my thoughts and Scriptures the Lord gave me:

Tonight, Lord, this Scripture has lightened the dark area of unbelief in my mind. It has penetrated the fear of poverty!

He humbled you, causing you to hunger and then feeding you with manna, which neither you nor your fathers had known, to teach you that man does not live on bread alone but on every word that comes from the mouth of the Lord....But remember the Lord your God, for it is He who gives you the ability to produce wealth, and so confirms His covenant... (Deuteronomy 8:3,18 NIV).

Conclusion—God has given me something that will produce wealth.

I penned the following prayer in desperation and pain:

Lord, what have You given me? What, Lord? What? Sales ability? Teaching ability? Preaching anointing? Craftsmanship? Artistic creativity? All these and more—but which one is meant to produce wealth? Father, I need to know Your divine guidance and wisdom. You know the right choices for me. I depend on you. You want me to provide an inheritance for my grandchildren, my wife, and family—this I know by Your own words in Proverbs. Now, Lord, lead me into the right opportunity and help me develop that [gift] which You have given me! I want to do nothing but Your will [in my life].

Almost two weeks later, the answer God gave rather shocked me.

JANUARY 28, 2000

My morning devotion.

God, the Holy Spirit, is asking me today: What's more important to you—to know *what* the gift I have given you is, or to know the *Giver* of the gift?

To have the gift I have given you, or to have the Giver of the gift with you, and within you?

To use the gift I have given you, or to obey the Giver of the gift?

I'm not so concerned about your offering yourself in service to Me as I am in knowing your fellowship and being with you! I don't want your offerings of money! I want you! Do you want to run off in ministry without My presence, My Holy Spirit to empower your efforts and to guide your works? [No, Lord, no!] Knowing My will is easy only when you know Me intimately, and you can know Me intimately only if you spend time with Me, listening to Me [in My Word]. You and your spouse, Cindy, would leave the house, go your separate ways, do your own work, which limited the time you had opportunity to talk to each other. On the contrary, I will not leave you, not do My own thing, not follow My own desires, even while you try to please Me while doing your own thing. No! I will stay with you and enable you to do the difficult and the simple things in your day's work. *So nothing shall be impossible for you!* I promise to always be with you. But if you resist My will, pursue your own ideas and desires, hurt Me or offend Me, I will be forced to withdraw [a space] from you and to wait, watching and hoping for the moment you will open your arms and welcome Me and My wisdom back into your life. As I wait, I will feel much like the way you feel about Cindy's rejecting you! In fact, it has been like this for Me already. There have been so many days I have longed for and hoped you would return to our place of intimacy, for My love to be showered on you, for us to share our thoughts together, so you might search Me as I search your heart also. It will become easy for you to know My will and My desires, My plan for your life when we continually commune with each other. It will be "second nature" for you. In fact, at some point, the old ways will pass away, and My nature will be first and foremost in control. I long for that moment when you are completely and wholly Mine, just as you long for that day to arrive [again] for you and Cindy. This is why I have allowed you to experience separation from the bride of your youth, the one you love, that you might cherish the days we spend alone and the moments we commune together just like the past moments you imagine and remember with Cindy. I remember those precious times with you as well! See how much more I long for you to surrender to Me than for your service to Me?

Yes, I also need your service and commitment, for I would not know your love was true without these works of obedience!

MY THOUGHTS MEASURED BY THE WORD OF GOD

My dad taught me that the Word of God is the only reliable standard for measuring the truths and belief systems that we allow to govern our choices in life. Every "spiritual encounter" we experience and religious teaching we adopt is to be judged by that Word of God before we allow it to "rent space in our heads." Our hearts might fool us, our minds might lead us astray, and our wills might be tainted by selfish desires; hence, we must always hold fast to God's Word, which cannot be changed. The excerpts from my diary might be tainted by human understanding, but I have found no Scripture that contradicts what I heard God saying to me when you consider the context in which it came.

Does God ever withdraw from us? Ultimately, God declares that He will never leave us nor forsake us (see Heb. 13:5). Indeed, nothing can ever separate us from the love of God (see Rom. 8:35-39). God is always close; we are never out of arms' reach. Yet His Word also declares that, "If we draw near to Him, He will draw near to us" (see James 4:8), implying that it is possible to separate ourselves from Him. I believe this Scripture speaks of our sensitivity to His proximity, our awareness of His closeness. It can be sharpened, or dulled, so that although He is right there with us, we might never know it!

GOD'S DIVINE PURPOSE

Our Father always practices good parenting skills. So when it comes to governing our lives and disciplining His children, He is always there. Furthermore, God has a divine purpose in the process of our learning and relearning the principles, precepts, and laws of God that govern our lives. We find it described by Paul in Romans:

> *Present your bodies a living sacrifice, holy, acceptable, to God, which is your reasonable service* [a reasonable act and response of love]. *And do not be conformed to this world, but be **transformed by the renewing of your mind, that you may prove what is that good and acceptable and perfect will of God*** (Romans 12:1b-2 NKJV).

God is always leading us to a greater revelation of His will and His purpose for our own lives as well as for His corporate family, the true Church. It starts with our understanding and receiving the *Good News* and the *goodness* of salvation. Then it progresses to where we learn to walk in freedom from condemnation when we stumble, and we no longer struggle to *accept* and love others, as Christ loves them. Finally, it progresses to where we are able to walk in His *perfect* will for our lives. This is the place where we walk in obedience to our purpose and calling. Sin has lost its attraction, while obedience and pleasing God appeals to our hearts. We are mature and able to understand the deeper, meatier truths in His Word. During this process, we will experience many things in life, and how they affect us will largely depend on us. We choose to win or lose the challenges, to grow in them or to blow it.

The first step is to recognize God's hand and work in our lives versus the world's influences. The world is always demanding conformation, while God is leading us into transformation. Conformation requires us to do little or nothing other than to accept the continual degrading and relaxing of our moral standards. It involves discarding the truth and believing the lies. Unfortunately, we often quit resisting the lies (in our schools for example) and accept the humanistic view, based on evolutionist theories, which says there is no God and the world and all living things are the result of a random and accidental series of events. They have tried to convince us to believe that we are continually evolving into a higher form of being with greater understanding, a wiser and more intelligent mankind. But the error of man's foolish ways are declared in the Word:

> *Claiming to be wise, they became utter fools instead....*
> *Instead of believing what they knew was the truth about*
> *God, they deliberately chose to believe lies. So they wor-*
> *shiped the things God made but not the Creator Him-*
> *self, who is to be praised forever (Romans 1:22,25).*

They deliberately forget that God made the heavens by the word of His command, and He brought the earth out from the water and surrounded it with water. Then He used the water to destroy the ancient world with a mighty flood (2 Peter 3:5-6).

It is so easy to conform simply through our silent assent and to go along with the lies; on the other hand, we can resist the temptation to relax and we can refuse to do nothing. We can transform our lives by willfully choosing to continually renew our mind and our thought patterns, by changing our habitual responses to the things that bombard us daily, and by aligning how we think and act with the truth God reveals in His Word. His Word declares that you can do all things through Christ who strengthens you (see Phil. 4:13). By His power, the power of the Holy Spirit within you, which was deposited within you when you were saved by His grace (see Eph. 1:13-14), you can do anything He asks of you. Yes, you *can* choose to say, think, and do those things that agree with what God declares in His Word and thus experience true transformation in this life. You can experience a true intimacy with your heavenly Father that grows deeper, purer, higher, and more meaningful as every day passes. The tough times can be that factor that compels you to seek God's heart, to gaze on His face, and feel His touch. But why wait and be a rainy-day Christian, when you can be a sunny-day saint who soaks up His love regardless of the circumstances you find yourself in?

As we close this chapter, the following prayer by Paul for the church in Ephesus is also my prayer for you and what you can experience in your life.

I pray that out of His glorious riches He may strengthen you with power through His Spirit in your inner being, so that Christ may dwell in your hearts through faith. And I pray that you, being rooted and established in love, may have power, together with all the saints, to grasp how wide and long and high and deep is the love of Christ, and to know this love that surpasses knowledge—that you may be filled to the measure of all the fullness of God. Now to Him who is able to do immeasurably more than all we ask or imagine, according to His power that is at work within us, to Him be glory in the church and in Christ Jesus throughout all generations, for ever and ever! Amen (Ephesians 3:16-21 NIV).

CHAPTER 5

Closing the Doors to Demons

The words of today often have very different meanings than they did 100, 50, or even 20 years ago. There was a time while I was growing up that "grass" was something that was mowed weekly, not smoked; "gay" was a perfectly acceptable state of happiness; "broad" meant the width of something; and "rad" was what helped cool the engine of your car. Today, the title "Christian" can also have a wide range of meanings.

Throughout this book, when I use the term "Christian," I am referring to a person who has placed his or her faith in the redemptive work of Christ on the cross, is aware of the lost state of humanity and their own soul without Christ, has repented and asked God to forgive them of their sin, has invited Christ to come into their heart and life, and whose primary purpose in life is to serve Christ as their Lord and King.

"Demon possessed" is another term that can mean different things to different people. While growing up, I recall that there were different views regarding what the Bible taught about the devil's influence on a Christian. There were and still are two extreme theological positions or beliefs about demonic possession of Christians. The one view says it is impossible for a Christian to be demon possessed and almost ignores spiritual warfare altogether. The other view states that Christians can be possessed; those extremists and adamant supporters of this view tend to run around casting demons out of everything or everyone who disagrees with them. The truth as usual is found somewhere in between the extremes.

EVIL FORCES WORK THROUGH HIDDEN MOTIVES

Error comes from a misunderstanding and misuse of the commonly used term, "demon possessed." This terminology tends to imply that a spirit is possessed by a demon. While this might be true for a non-Christian, I don't believe it is true for a Christian. A proper term and one that is correctly rendered from the Greek term *daimonizomai* would be "demonization," which signifies that one is "acting under the influence and control of a demon." It really boils down to a state or condition of the soul, not the spirit. That a believer can be influenced by demonic activity or controlled by demonic forces is evidenced quite strongly by the words of Christ to Peter in Matthew chapter 16. Previously, Jesus had prophesied His own death in the near future.

> *But Peter took Him aside and corrected Him. "Heaven forbid, Lord," he said. "This will never happen to You!" Jesus turned to Peter and said, "Get away from Me, satan! You are a dangerous trap to Me. You are seeing things merely from a human point of view, and not from God's." Then Jesus said to the disciples, "If any of you wants to be My follower, you*

*must put aside your **selfish ambition**, shoulder your cross, and follow Me"* (Matthew 16:22-24).

When we examine the situation and time frame of this Scripture, we find that this conversation occurred only shortly after Peter had openly confessed that Jesus was the Messiah, the Christ, and also some time after the twelve disciples had returned from being sent out to preach the Good News, heal the sick, and cast out demons.

Was Peter a Christian by scriptural standards? I believe he was, based on his professed faith in the person and work of Jesus Christ rather than on what Peter had been doing. Peter's actions were profoundly remarkable by this time in his walk as a disciple of Christ. He had left his lifelong profession and career as a successful fisherman, walked on water, cast out demons, recruited followers, and experienced the multiplication miracle of loaves and fishes in his own hands as he distributed their meager resources. But in the midst of his good works and his honorable intentions, there was an evil force trying to work through him. It is apparent that it gained access through his hidden motives, which Jesus identified as "selfish ambition." Good works and incredible actions are clearly not what qualify anyone for eternal life in Heaven. Referring to eternity, Jesus Himself said,

> *On judgment day many will tell Me, "Lord, Lord, we prophesied in Your name and cast out demons in Your name and performed many miracles in Your name." But I will reply, "I never knew you. Go away..."* (Matthew 7:22-23).

Our citizenship in Heaven is based on our confession of faith in Jesus as the Christ, the Messiah, and Lord and Savior; and our willingness to follow, obey, and serve Christ the Lord as our Master. Clearly, Peter had been following, obeying, and serving the Master just before this incident where he was rebuked by Christ for serving selfish ambition. James, the brother of Christ, also gives a clear warning about our motives:

> For *wherever there is jealousy and selfish ambition, there you will find disorder and every kind evil* (James 3:16).

This passage is directed to Christians and is part of instructions warning them of the evil and destructive power of their words. Listen to the advice that precedes this Scripture:

> *But if you are bitterly jealous and there is selfish ambition in your hearts, don't brag about being wise. That is the worst kind of lie. For jealousy and selfishness are not God's kind of wisdom. Such things are earthly, unspiritual, and motivated by the devil* (James 3:14-15).

So when Jesus addressed Peter in the manner He did, He was speaking to an evil spirit that was motivating Peter's flesh with selfish ambition and attitudes.

Can Christians be influenced and controlled by demons or evil spirits? Yes, I believe they can be, when there is a doorway of opportunity through which the spirit or demons can gain access. Does this mean they have lost their salvation and are heading to hell? I don't believe that was what James was teaching at all. He was warning us to be on the alert, to be aware of the dangers of rejecting the truth concerning our own soul, and to be conscious of the attitudes and evil motives that can be hidden or tucked away within us.

While we are stationed on the front lines in a battle to expand the Kingdom of God on this earth, we must be careful that we do not allow our hearts and desires to be overcome with anything that this world offers as rewards. When we entertain selfish desires or thoughts, we are drawn away from God's will; and these thoughts grow into lusts, which begin to control and influence our actions. These actions become sin, and when left to mature, can bring death to us (see James 1:14-15). When we least expect it, they surface and trip us up or wound a weaker brother or sister and render us both ineffective in the warfare we are called to be a part of on this earth.

MAN'S DOMINION OVER SATAN ON EARTH

To truly understand why Christians continue to battle with the sins of their own pasts, generational curses, or the result of experiences such as our mothers had while we were yet in their womb, we must first understand the makeup of a person's entire being.

First and foremost, we are made in the image of God.

Then God said, "Let Us make man in Our image, according to Our likeness; let them have dominion over the fish of the sea, over the birds of the air, and over the cattle, over all the earth and over every creeping thing that creeps on the earth." So God created man in His own image; in the image of God He created him; male and female He created them (Genesis 1:26-27 NKJV).

I have heard many explanations of this passage, but none agrees with the Scripture better or makes more sense to me than that we are created to look like God and act like God, and as the verses indicate, to have dominion like God—that is, dominion over all that God created on this earth. However, this does not mean we can become God. We were created to fellowship with God, worship Him, and to serve as His ambassadors and ruling force over His creation. We were designed and created to be creative, multiply, and fill the entire earth, and to bring all things created here on earth under our subjection (see Gen. 1:28). This dominion also included power over lucifer or satan who was roaming the earth where he had been banished by God at some point in time following creation. Psalms explains our position as beings in God's order as *a little lower than the angels"* (Ps. 8:5-6 NKJV).

But sometime after we were created, lucifer and his accomplices revolted and became fallen angels, no longer holding authority over anything except those whom they could subdue by default or ignorance. Their domain was the "air" or "heavenlies," a reference to the spiritual realm over which they held dominance or authority on this earth (see Eph. 2:2; 6:12). Lucifer's authority was limited to the fallen angelic beings that were cast down to this planet with him, which he ruled over, using fear, intimidation, coercing, pain, abuse, and manipulation. He continues to be restricted to the realm or confines of earth's material or natural space or atmosphere (the first heaven). Whereas, entering the realm of God's presence or His throne room (the third heaven) is something he can do only while the "sons of God" or "children of God gather together." His prison has been defined by the natural confines of earth's atmosphere and the unseen spiritual realm that exists within the same. In short, he can no longer roam the other planets, moons, stars, galaxies, or universe (the second heaven). He is confined to the same space geographically as we are (except perhaps when we leave this earth's orbit and head for the moon). (See the story in the first two chapters of the Book of Job.)

So, within the parameters of this space that he has been banished to, he has lost his deceptive abilities and influence which he had previously used to rally some one third of the heavenly spiritual forces. The other two thirds—cherubs, seraphim, and archangels who had *not* succumbed to his lies and joined in his first rebellion and who had already resisted his beguiling ways—quite possibly could not be seduced or deceived by him from then on. His deceptive ways had been exposed to them by the Father, and they were secure walking in the light and truth that protected them from any of his further attempts to win them over to his side.

In the Book of Job, we find that satan made an appearance before God when the *"sons of God came to present themselves before the Lord"* (see Job 1:6; 2:1 NKJV). I have always questioned how satan was allowed to go before God's throne if he had been banished to this earth. But one day, my pastor, speaking on this passage, reminded us that the term "sons of God" is used in reference to the saints, the children of Israel, as well as angels. So, this passage could mean that satan had slipped into a worship service or prayer meeting. When gatherings are held and practiced all over the world in public or in secret places by the saints and the Church, we are joined by the Holy Spirit (God) and also angels, undoubtedly. The Book of Matthew declares:

> *For where two or three are gathered together in My name, I am there in the midst of them* (Matthew 18:20 NKJV).

I believe these gatherings are the only occasion where satan can come before the presence of God! It's the third heaven touching earth! It's significant that Jesus talked about people meeting together in His name while He was also teaching about the power to bind and loose, and the power of agreement. His statement also preceded His teaching on forgiveness. I think He was trying to emphasize the authority and power we have in the spiritual "third heaven" realm as we truly walk in freedom and forgiveness.

However, while able to visit this same "third heaven" realm that Paul makes reference to in Second Corinthians 12:2, satan is rendered powerless and holds no ability to exhibit dominion except in those whom he has gained access to by rights they have defaulted to him. It is apparent from the Scriptures that while on this earth, he retains his supernatural ability to transform himself, to inspire worshippers to worship, and to manipulate the natural elements on earth to some degree. He can also inflict pain or disease, cause natural disasters and storms, manipulate substance or material, and wreak havoc in our lives, given the right circumstances. But we must remember, he is not omnipresent (everywhere at all times), omniscient (all-knowing), or omnipotent (all-powerful). He might try to get you to believe that he is, but he's not.

Moreover, I believe that prior to the fall of Adam and Eve, he was far more limited in his ability to harm or control humanity. He gained his authority and influence by deceiving Eve and Adam into forfeiting the place they had been given by God on earth as the dominant creation. From the time satan was cast out of his heavenly place, he has hated God and anything or anyone God has created. He suffers from the greatest "rejection complex" of all time, and he seeks to destroy and devour anything that reminds him of what he lost when God rejected him and cast him out of His presence. The most prized element of his prior position I believe was his fellowship in the throne room with God. Satan is extremely jealous of what we have been created to do—fellowship with the Most High God in the heavens. His highest aim is to rob from us the very thing he has lost, and to cause us to ultimately be rejected before God also. We, on the other hand, despite our fallen nature and loss of freedom to fellowship with the Father for eternity, have been given a second opportunity to fulfill the destiny and purposes of God on this earth for which we were created for in the beginning.

DOING WHAT WE WERE CREATED TO DO

We, the Church, have a corporate destiny. Each of us also has a personal destiny or purpose, which God is working to restore to us as we spend time in fellowship with Him. On the other hand, satan's ultimate goal is to steal our destiny, rob us of purpose, and prevent earth and Heaven from becoming more populated with human beings who serve God with total devotion and obedience. Even though he has already been outnumbered in the great battle in the spiritual realm—two to one, I suspect he has been trying from the first day of creation, to keep that disadvantage from getting any worse—specifically, by recruiting men and women, even children to do his work unknowingly for him.

The spiritual realm is not a peaceful place on earth. It is in constant upheaval and havoc. And undeniably, satan will win some battles from time to time in homes, societies, political arenas, or in the realms of merchants and marketplaces. He might win a few skirmishes as he influences political leaders, kings, governments, or military regimes, ruling over countries, regions, provinces, people groups, or other segments of society; but ultimately, he will lose any power he has retained on this earth. In the meantime, He is a real sore loser and wants to take down as many of God's beloved creation with him to the pit he is destined for. His methods are varied and many, and he is always delighted when he can thwart or waylay God's children from walking in the purposes that God has created them to fulfill on the earth.

Therefore, in order to be the greatest threat to satan's kingdom, we must have a song in our hearts and praise on our lips. Worship is the warfare, and praise is the artillery that defeats the enemy every time. Keeping an attitude of gratitude and a heart of humility and submission to God's work and will for us, will close the door to demonic influence every time!

The secret to joy-filled living is to discover the specific work or task God has designed us for, and do it. We are always our happiest and most effective when we do what we were created to do. The Book of Jeremiah makes this clear to us.

> *"Before I made you in your mother's womb, I chose you. Before you were born, I set you apart for a special work"* (Jeremiah 1:5 NCV).

> *"For I know the plans I have for you," says the Lord. "They are plans for good and not for disaster, to give*

you a future and a hope. In those days when you pray, I will listen. If you look for me wholeheartedly, you will find me. I will be found by you," says the Lord. "I will end your captivity and restore your fortunes" (Jeremiah 29:11-14a).

Walking in God's purpose puts a gladness in our hearts, a strength in our bones, and a song on our lips. It gives determination, removes fears and doubts, and sets the course of our days ahead. It is serving in the place God has called you to serve. It's more than a job; it's more than a career; it's a vocation and calling. Fredrich Buechner said it this way: "The place God calls you to is the place where your deep gladness and the world's deep hunger meet."[1] Happy and joy-filled Christians, with the love and peace of God ruling their lives, are a powerful drawing force to those who have empty and pain-filled lives.

WALKING IN GOD'S PURPOSE
PUTS A GLADNESS IN OUR HEARTS,
A STRENGTH IN OUR BONES,
AND A SONG ON OUR LIPS.

We each are created to fill a void or a place that God designed us to fill perfectly. Finding your vocation is less about discovering your occupation than about uncovering your preoccupation. When you do discover or uncover it, you become one of God's greatest assets and the devil's greatest enemy. You will impact his realm to such an extent that your reputation will precede you, much the same as it did for the apostle Paul.

A team of Jews who were traveling from town to town casting out evil spirits tried to use the name of the Lord Jesus. The incantation they used was this: "I command you by Jesus, whom Paul preaches, to come out!" Seven sons of Sceva, a leading priest, were doing this. But when they tried it on a man possessed by an evil spirit, the spirit replied, "I know Jesus, and I know Paul. But who are you?" (Acts 19:13-15)

Paul was well-known in the spirit realm, and so it should be with each of us.

When each of us was born on earth, it was into a spiritual environment of jealousy, torment, anger, pride, wickedness, rebellion, abuse, and every evil means that satan uses to torment and maintain his rule over spirits or angels that fell from their place in Heaven with him, as well as over men and women who are serving his purposes unwittingly. But we don't need to live under the false authority of the demon squatters who have tried to keep the territory that Christ has removed from their control on the cross. We can take back what is rightfully ours once again.

The next time that the enemy comes knocking to try to rob your possessions or strip your inheritance, be determined to walk in your authority, kick his butt out the door and off your property, and slam the door behind him. Don't worry if it bangs into his butt on the way out. We're supposed to put him under our feet anyway.

ENDNOTE

1. Fredrich Buechner, *Wishful Thinking* (San Francisco, CA: Harper San Francisco, 1993), 119.

CHAPTER 6

He's Got His Father's Eyes

*Then God said, "Let **Us** make man in **Our** image..."*
(Genesis 1:26 NKJV).

Have you ever watched moms flock around a new arrival in the infant nursery? If you've listened to the comments and observations from friends and acquaintances, they probably went something like this:

"Oh my! What a doll! She looks just like you!"

"Isn't he a looker. He's so perfect. And he's got his father's gorgeous blue eyes!"

(You guessed it—I've got blue eyes.)

Well, that statement doesn't make sense to most of the older kids hanging around. If he's really got his father's eyes that would make his father blind! But when it comes to babies, every

91

loving mom and dad is blind anyway...love is always blind to imperfections, right?

But here's the point: We are made in the image of God. We look like our Father, and this is especially true for newborn babies, I believe. Perhaps that's why people are drawn to babies like iron is to magnets.

Why do babies carry a greater resemblance to God than say, a pimply-faced, greasy-haired, buck-toothed, 13-year-old boy? It's because of their innocence and perfection. As human beings we are never more alive than when we take our first breath! But from the moment we enter this world, our bodies begin to suffer death and dying. Even our skin begins to die, and the dead skin cells slough off into the air around us. A-a-argh! So from the time I was a kid growing up, I've been breathing in my smelly sisters and my neighbor's aging grandma! Disgusting thought, I'm sure! But it's true. (No, not the part about my sisters being smelly. Most eight-year-old boys think that about girls for a short season.) And the older we get, the more difficult time our bodies have in replacing the dying cells. Furthermore, as we become weighed down by the cares of this world, the dying process speeds up; consequently, we look even less like our Father. To be sure, the closest thing we'll ever know to a Garden-of-Eden body is our first few breaths as babies.

IN THE IMAGE OF THE TRIUNE GOD

When life on earth began for us as God's creation and prior to our original sin (Eve and Adam eating the fruit), we looked far more like Him than we really understand today. Undoubtedly, satan did not appreciate a living creature walking this earth who looked like God. Most probably, it reminded him daily of all that he had lost. Furthermore, it soon became evident that God had put this creation in charge of the earth. We were created in the image of God, and we were vessels that housed the glory of God. I believe the term "image of God" or our likeness to the Godhead encompasses more than the bipedal physical form we were designed in. Please note that I make reference to the Godhead—the triune God who declared, *"Let Us make man in Our image..."* (Genesis 1:26a NKJV).

The plurality of the persons of God is represented in the term "Us." God was talking to His Son and to the Holy Spirit, and They were discussing what kind of creature They should create that would rule over and dominate this earth. They wanted something or someone who would clearly represent Them on earth, someone with whom They could fellowship, relate to, and who would come to an understanding of Them. These three personalities and beings who form one God considered Their uniqueness as being three yet one, and determined how Their creation could best represent Them in a form for which all three could enjoy and recognize the key aspect of Their individuality and personalities. The end result of Their choice was that man should also be a three-part being—a trichotomy. This discussion can be quite challenging to grasp; therefore, I'll elaborate so that you can think it through.

First, to best represent the Father, he was given a soul, made up of the mind, will, and emotions. He became his own person, housing a personality unique to himself, an individual with a mind of his own from which he could exercise and experience free will, creativity, a hunger, a thirst for fellowship and companionship, and a wide range of emotions from anger to love.

Second, to represent the Son, he was given a physical body and shape that represented a likeness to the form of the Son of God, Jesus Christ, which He chose when He revealed Himself on earth to creation. Just as Jesus Christ has always given up His own desires to do the work and fulfill the will of the Father, likewise our body will only do what our brain, mind, and will instruct it to do. Our bodies are subject to our will by design, just as Christ was subject to the Father's will by choice (see John 8:29).

Third, to represent the Holy Spirit, the Father breathed into His creation the breath or wind of the Spirit. He placed in seed form the essence of His Spirit, thus enabling mankind to commune with Him "in the spirit." Life begat life! Spirit begat spirit! We were made with the creative force of God in us. Do not confuse this terminology with the new age terminology used in reference to the nonpersonal force many express they believe is everywhere and can be manipulated to serve their own purpose. The Holy Spirit has power beyond comprehension, which is exhibited in many ways in this world. He is not simply some form of energy. He is a distinct personality who wants only to exalt and serve the purposes and will of the Father while residing in His children and on the earth. It is this unique and distinct aspect within us that gives us eternal life and sets us apart from all other created and living things.

A SPIRITUAL CANCER

After the fall of man, our spirits became corrupted by sin and death, and we became a slave to the flesh, to serve our own selfish desires and our own wills. When Adam and Eve sinned, they willfully took away from the Holy Spirit the seat of authority in their hearts that He had occupied. They no longer yielded their wills to the Father but sought to satisfy their own desires, which were in conflict with the Father's. This is the root or essence of the spirit of disobedience as it took residence within them. The evidence is still in us today. The highest drive within each of us even as brand-new babies is self-preservation and self-gratification. No wonder Jesus declared that there was no greater display of the presence of God's love within a man than when he or she is willing to lay down their life for a friend. The greatest example of God in control of human nature is when a Christian denies the self-preservation instinct and gives his life for a stranger or even an enemy! I believe from creation until the fall, Adam and Eve both would have sacrificed their lives for one another. But after the fall of Eve and Adam, something changed; and it soon became evident within their sons's lives. Cain became filled with pride, jealousy, and murderous anger when God accepted his brother Abel's sacrifice but rejected his own (see Gen. 4:1-15). Later, James wrote:

> *For jealousy and selfishness are not God's kind of wisdom. Such things are earthly, unspiritual, and motivated by the devil. For wherever there is jealousy and selfish ambition, there you will find disorder and every kind of evil* (James 3:15-16).

This jealousy and selfishness became an open doorway for satan to do what he does best, and to influence Cain to kill and destroy God's creation that He was so pleased with. The plot to destroy mankind had taken a giant leap forward as the first murder transpired. I think of this sin factor as spiritual cancer. The corruption became contagious and irreversible, and once it infiltrated humanity, it was passed on from generation to generation.

There is only one way to deal with the corruption or cancer, and that is to have an operation that gives you a new spirit. God removes the corrupt and dead spirit that is incapable of communion with God, and replaces it with one that is "alive unto Him" when you are born again. Without this operation, you will never regain the ability to fellowship with the Father. It would be like trying to get an old computer from the early 60's to connect to a state-of-the-art laptop computer today. They simply are not compatible—they don't speak the same language, nor do they have the necessary ports to connect. The operation needed is the salvation that Christ has given to us by dying on the cross. Our "spiritual DNA" can be restored back to what God had originally created in us through God's redeeming power of the cross.

HIDDEN STONES IN THE SOUL

For some people, this Good News is so easy to accept and understand, and they begin to change immediately. Their lives soon exhibit the fruit of the Spirit, and they are transformed. Whereas, there are others who also believe and receive the Good News with joy, but within a short time, they fall away and even deny that they had experienced anything supernatural at all. What causes the difference between the two and prevents the second one from growing spiritually?

Have you ever driven by the same farmer's prairie fields year after year? Perhaps you have noticed how the rocks and stones that lie buried below the surface soil of the farmer's field appear every spring and need to be removed yearly before planting a crop. It's almost like someone scattered pebbles over the field in the fall and come spring...voila, you have a fresh crop of stones and rocks. However, it doesn't work like that. The stones were actually dropped and buried beneath the soil during the ice age as the ice fields were retreating and melting away. They lay buried beneath the soil many feet below the surface. As season after season transpires, the frost pushes the stones ever closer to the surface. Many farmers have damaged and broken good plow blades on rocks that are still hidden just under the surface soil. Moreover, these rocks hinder the planting process and keep the field from yielding the full potential of harvest unless removed. I've seen some fields so badly laden with rocks, they were impossible to use for planting and harvesting; and I've watched farmers diligently remove pile after pile of rocks every year, yet it seemed as though they had not touched the field at all. In England, for centuries these rocks have been harvested, piled on the property lines between the landowner's fields and now form three to four–foot high walls that need gateways or openings to allow passage through.

There are people whose hearts and souls are like these unattended fields. If the Gospel is to take root in them and have a transforming effect, they will need a divine miracle. Jesus used the parable of the sower and the seed to illustrate why some people seem to hear the Good News or the Word of God, yet it has almost no lasting personal effect or permanent change; while others hear and their lives are transformed into wonderfully fruitful places filled with God's blessings and joy. Jesus explained the stony ground in Matthew chapter 13:

> *The rocky soil represents those who hear the message and receive it with joy. But like young plants in such soil, their roots don't go very deep. At first they get along fine, but they wilt as soon as they have problems or are persecuted because they believe the word* (Matthew 13:20-21).

Do you notice what it is that keeps them from having strength of soul and faith to withstand the storms of life and persecution for their faith? It is the hidden rocks or deep-rooted soul issues. These are internal personal problems within our own soul. They are often identity issues, which include self-esteem, self-assurance in knowing who we are, unforgiveness, jealousy, bitterness, childhood fears that still grip us, and anything that cripples the power of God's Word from transforming us or prevents us from growing into fruitful members of God's Kingdom. People who truly have a sense of who they are and of their purpose and place in life are not easily swayed by ridicule or persecution from others around them who disagree with them.

Now, there will come persecution because of our believing in God's Word, but whether we are able to stand through that testing period depends entirely on the condition of the soil of our soul. Is it full of stones and rocks that keep the Word from rooting deeply within us? Satan will always use fear, unbelief, or doubts to rob us of the blessings God intended for us to walk in as we fulfill His purpose for our lives. Thus, if we are to harvest a crop of God's blessing in our own lives, we need to remove or deal with the hidden issues that lay hidden deep in our hearts or souls. We do so by putting ourselves in a position where we invite the Holy Spirit to examine us and reveal our hearts so that we are able to address the issues that are there. David asked God to inspect his own heart; his prayer is recorded in Psalm 139:23-24:

> *Search me, O God, and know my heart; test me and know my anxious thoughts* [reveal my hidden motives, drives, intentions]. *Point out anything in me that offends You, and lead me along the path of everlasting life* (Psalm 139:23-24).

Unfortunately, these issues are often left there undealt with until they pop up to be stumbled over by some unsuspecting soul. In time, they become the building materials for walls that keep out God's blessings or a stronghold from which the enemy launches attack after attack against us in our lives.

"LORD, REVEAL THOSE HIDDEN AND HAUNTING ROCKS"

Who allows these root issues to remain in us and thwart God's purposes? We do. Even though we turned our past lives and futures over to Christ when we were saved, we must also continue to allow Him to deal with our past issues *if* they are still keeping us from growing to spiritual maturity. Much of our past will never need to be brought up again nor should be, because we have given it to Christ and His blood and grace has covered it and dealt with it. However, once in a while, God will bring something to our memory so that He can deal with it. This is necessary because in the past we might have unconsciously closed the doors to certain memories or wounds that are still controlling our lives today. While these past issues are under the blood and forgiven because we have consciously turned our lives over to Christ, we still might have "pushed them under the rug" or "locked them away in a closet" to hide them while Christ was trying to do some serious housecleaning in our lives. What I mean by that is— we might well have held back from opening the psychological "door to the closet" where those painful memories or offences were tucked away to allow us to cope with life after we were wounded. Sometimes, when certain memories surface, they bring anger, jealousy, envy, bitterness, deep pain, paralyzing fear, or intense regret; and many times they are rooted in unforgiveness. These need to be turned over to Christ and dealt with.

For God's grace is so awesome and so limitless; and I'm convinced that it is greater than our hearts when we have tried to protect ourselves from pain. He sees the deepest part of us and understands the human psyche better than we ourselves. First John 3:20 tells us:

> For if our heart condemn us, God is greater than our heart, and knoweth all things (1 John 3:20 KJV).

This promise can bring extraordinary peace and hope for those who are being filled with doubts that they are saved because of the struggles they've been having. The key to sorting out this dilemma of dealing with the past that's been forgiven but still haunts us with regret, pain, fear, or unforgiveness is found in the desire that God puts within us. When our desires are to please God, walk in forgiveness, and to be free to serve Him wholeheartedly, we can be rest assured that He is still working in us and that we are saved by grace. It is the occasion where *"The spirit indeed is willing, but the flesh is weak"* (Mark 14:38b NKJV).

However, when we get into the realm of self-justification for our unforgiving attitude toward others, bitterness that demands revenge, or envy that drives our ambitions to a place where we hurt others to get what we want regardless of the consequences, we are approaching dangerous territory. It is when He repeatedly has warned us over and over again and we have absolutely refused to listen to God's voice or heed His warnings that we soon find ourselves on that slippery slope of rebellion that leads to destruction. We will examine this subject in subsequent chapters.

But before you read further, why not take a moment to pray and ask the Father to reveal anything hidden deep within you that may be keeping you from thriving with abundance of fruit and blessing.

Regarding David, the Bible says,

David, a man about whom God said, "David son of Jesse a man after My own heart. He will do everything I want him to do" (Acts 13:22b).

Try praying what David prayed:

"Search me, O God, and know my heart; test me and know my anxious thoughts. Point out anything in me that offends You, and lead me along the path of everlasting life" (Psalm 139:23-24).

That's a great place to start!

CHAPTER 7

The Building Blocks of Strongholds

Sometime during the past eight years of my life, I have learned that the enemy of our souls secretly seeks to gain a foothold in us from which he entrenches his position until he ultimately develops a stronghold. The first time I began to realize just how much these strongholds can remain hidden within us was when God revealed that I was carrying an unnecessary burden of shame, which had its roots of deception in my childhood. These root issues kept me trapped in a continuous cycle of defeat and failure, while slowly eroding the foundations of my marriage, setting it up for destruction.

REGRETS, SHAME, AND THE POWER OF FORGIVENESS

In the summer of 1995, I was pastor of a small church in Bashaw, Alberta, Canada, to which I would travel an hour and a half biweekly to minister to our growing little congregation. During the days, I held a full-time job while spending my evenings preparing Bible studies and messages. One week as I struggled to prepare for Sunday's message, I picked up Max Lucado's book, *He Still Moves Stones*, to get some inspiration for my soul. As I read the chapter entitled, "The Sack of Stones," I found the teaching, to say the least, profound, and somewhat of a difficult pill for me to swallow.

In this chapter, Max paints a picture of many Christians who battle regrets, guilt, shame, and haunting memories of past sins. He points out that while we agree with the message of the cross and believe that Christ died to take away all these burdens of the sinful nature, we still often fail to leave these sack of burdens, or stones as he puts it, at the foot of the cross where they belong. Instead, we set them down at the cross when we come into the church, then pick them up when we leave to carry on with our daily living outside the church. I remember thinking, *Now isn't that the truth. So many people have difficulty letting go of the past and letting Christ wipe away their sins. I'm glad I don't have that problem anymore and I know I'm forgiven.* Then I set the book down to go to bed.

That night I had a dream that greatly impacted my life; it altered my perspective completely, set me free, and implanted a deep personal desire to see others set free from similar bondages. The dream was directly from the Holy Spirit and shook me to the depth of my soul. I awoke at 5:00 A.M. with a strong sense of the presence of the Holy Spirit in the room. I then woke my wife up to tell her what God was showing me about my childhood and the shame I was still carrying from it. She was exhausted and encouraged me to go downstairs to the office and write it down so I wouldn't forget it and could share it with her tomorrow.

After listening to the Spirit for several minutes, I asked Him to please help me put the thoughts and truths on paper. I got up, and in my office I sat weeping as He spoke to me as a mother to her child. I wrote as quickly as I could between waves of revelation, memories, and convictions over the "sack of stones," and regret and shame that I had held within my soul for 30-some odd years. I released a lot of junk that night, then went to see my mom to deal with the way I had unconsciously been treating her. There was a great release of childhood shame and fears, and we were both set free through repentance and forgiveness.

During the message on the following Sunday, I related my experience and taught on the subject of regrets, shame, and the power of forgiveness. An altar call followed for those who felt God's Spirit speaking to them, and almost the entire congregation came forward to the altar. The anointing fell on us all, and many were set free, young and old. God led me through prophetic revelation to address sexual molestation, physical abuse, deep shame from lost innocence, and many other issues that were influencing the lives of those in my congregation. Many years later, the impact of that Sunday's ministry in their lives is still evident, and their testimonies report of that pivotal day when God showed up after first changing their pastor's heart.

THE WOUNDS ARE MANY

I tell the previous story to illustrate that you can be in the center of God's place for your life, serving Him faithfully, yet your impact can be severely limited because of events from your early childhood, or deep negative emotions passed into your soul even while in your mother's womb. There could be any number of things you have hidden beneath your conscious memory that affect your response to things that happen daily in your life. These events are often buried too deeply to recall at will, and when they inadvertently surface, they carry many feelings and painful emotions with them, evidence that they still need to be dealt with. Many psychiatrists are using various techniques to deal with hidden memories, some of which are dangerous, even ungodly, including hypnosis, auto-suggestion, role-play, regressive techniques, or associative aromas to stimulate memory recall. While some people receive help using certain techniques, other people might not yet be emotionally capable of dealing with the buried memories. Only God knows when it is safe to deal with these things and the best way to handle the process. His Holy Spirit is able to expose and heal safely in a few hours that which man *might* succeed in doing over several months or years, or perhaps never.

Recently, I read an account of the outpouring of the Holy Spirit on the Presbyterian Church in Indonesia during the late 60's and early 70's. The story was told by Mel Tari, an eyewitness who later was called to travel around the world to preach and share the Good News to many other countries. Mel Tari had not had much contact with Christians outside of the church on the island of Timor and had lived most of his life in the village of Soe near the capitol city of Kupang.

One year after his experience with the outpouring of the Holy Spirit, God told him he was to go to America. Because he had not traveled before this and was naïve concerning the western culture in America, he had the misconception that living in America must be like living in Heaven, for even inscribed on their money they declared that they put their trust in God. Of course, his eyes were opened after arriving. When praying for the Christians he ministered to in the American churches, the Lord revealed that many of our sicknesses, financial problems, and social issues were due to the hidden wounds that so many people carry. I quote from his own words in his book, *Like a Mighty Wind*:

> The more I have traveled in America, the more aware
> I have become that many people in the churches have

a brokenness or a wound because of past experiences. In the hearts of most Americans there is a bitterness, a hurt, or something. The result is that they feel bad inside and have no power or joy. In counselling many, I have discovered that this is something from their past, sometimes from their childhood or teenage years.[1]

His observation is so true. I have also become far more aware of these hidden wounds and the broken condition of many fellow Christians since my own experience. Many times I have looked into the eyes of people I am praying for, or Christians I meet in my daily life, or even strangers on the street, and I am made aware of their wounded hearts. I can often tell them when and where the root of their pain began. Sometimes I am shown a picture of them, or the Holy Spirit speaks in my ear and reveals to me what I am dealing with. I am convinced it is these things that have crippled the Church and opened the door for the enemy to rob, kill, and destroy our blessings and potential ministry of power from us. Satan does not want you to understand the significance of past events and painful emotions; they are his secret strongholds. He especially does not want you to believe they could impact the way you behave today or to understand that God longs to expose and destroy these hidden strongholds.

The dream that God gave me and the subsequent revelation of what was hidden in my heart began a fresh examination and evaluation of my life. I cried out as David did before the Lord.

Search me, O God, and know my heart: try me, and know my thoughts: and see if there be any wicked way in me, and lead me in the way everlasting (Psalm 139:23-24 KJV).

Thereafter, I experienced such a deep longing for God's presence and manifestation of His power in my ministry. I spent hours on my face before God, asking Him to direct my life and to make my life count for eternal values. Surely I became desperate to hear from Him and to be in the center of His will at all times, crying out for Him to do in me whatever was necessary to make me fit to serve Him as a worthy vessel for His anointing. *Nothing* else mattered to me except to fulfill His call on my life.

The following years became a series of events where God molded and prepared me to be the vessel that God had designed me to be. It was a process of building, tearing down, refining, and polishing off all the rough edges in my character that hindered me from fulfilling His call on my life. I had cried to Him to do whatever it took, and unknowingly I was to start down a road that was not at all what I expected to go through.

A NEW CALLING

After another year of ministry in Bashaw, I distinctly felt God directing me to resign my pastorate and seek out a work that would allow me the freedom to spend more time with my wife and family. The absence of my presence at home was taking a toll, and we came to understand that although we didn't want to leave our loving little church family, our work in Bashaw was done. We had taken this young church, which was a considerable distance from our home, as far as we could, and we had to trust God to bring someone who could take the work on from there.

In the meantime, I had no idea what God was preparing me for or what the future held for my wife and me. I sought a position of employment in Bashaw for several months, but no doors opened. Late that summer, I resigned from my position and began a prayerful search for an open church. After many weeks of sending out resumes, we heard that there was opening in a church in the community where we lived. Subsequently, we expressed a willingness to help the struggling church and submitted a resume to their board. We had been a part of this community for more than 15 years and were well-known there. In addition, we had a great love for our community and a deep burning desire to see a strong and vibrant church that would reach out to the "un-churched" crowd and the many single moms and dads who had been through divorces or never married but had a family to raise.

As we continued to wait for a response from the churches we had applied to, my wife also made a call to the Word of Life Church in Red Deer to investigate what kind of organization they were. Although we knew very little about the church, we had heard that their philosophy or doctrinal beliefs were quite similar to our own. After a lengthy set of questions, a pastoral staff member at that church recommended that we talk to their church planting director, Pastor Gary Carter, and within a few hours, we had an appointment to meet with him and his wife just a few days thereafter.

We met with them both on a Monday evening, and from the moment we shook hands, I sensed deep in my spirit that our destiny was directly linked to this organization, and more specifically to this pastor's ministry. By the time the evening was over, both my wife and I felt like the disciples on the Emmaus road. Our hearts burned with a desire to experience the things that were happening within this church and the Word of Life's fellowship of churches. The structure, philosophy, doctrine, and the way their organization's accountability structure operated fit our understanding and beliefs to a tee.

We were excited about the future possibilities, but before jumping into a relationship with this organization, we agreed to wait, pray, and see what God would do about the resume on the desk of the local church we were still attending. Our hearts were knit to the people there, and we longed that the existing work would acquire some strong leadership to keep it alive. We had a burden for the community, yet we were not certain that we were the ones called to lead that congregation. I wanted that witness in both of our hearts before making any commitments. So, we determined that we would let God open or close the door and show us the direction we were to take.

Within a day of our visit with Pastors Gary and Kim Carter, we received a call to attend a general meeting at our local church. Although we had not been attending there for the six consecutive months which their constitution required to have a voting voice, the board felt it was appropriate we be there because of our past association with the church and our present interest in being their pastors. The meeting was held two days later. We sat in the meeting listening to the options presented and the subsequent choices they made for their future. In the midst of this meeting, we were handed a letter that expressed their gratitude for our interest in the church, and their regrets that due to their present financial situation, they could not take us on as their pastors at that time.

When the meeting closed, we left feeling a heavy burden for the struggling church and a deep continuing desire to impact our community. We realized our vision for the type of church we felt the community desperately needed was not what this church had a vision for nor was it part of their purpose for being there. Figuratively speaking, we would have been trying to put "new wine into old wineskins," while God wants the "old wineskins" to remain intact and fulfill the purpose that they were placed in the community for in the first place. More and more, we felt like we had become sheep in the wrong fold. But God was about to change all that for us.

Before my wife and I retired that evening, we received a call from Pastor Gary Carter inquiring if we had been given a church to pastor. When we related the outcome of the meeting with our local church, he asked the question that set our lives on a whole new path. "Are you ready to plant a new work with us in Fort Saskatchewan?" We learned a few months later that the Word of Life churches had already been scoping out the Fort and had been praying about planting a work there before we had called. Our call was providential and Spirit led.

GOD SPEAKS LOUD AND CLEAR

Immediately, we started a home prayer meeting in Fort Saskatchewan and began the process of acquiring the necessary training and team to start a new church under the covering of Pastor Gary Carter, Pastor Mel Mullen, and the Word of Life churches. We held our first public service on January 4, 1997, and again one week later in a wonderful facility God had graciously provided at very inexpensive rates.

My first message was about receiving a vision from God and making resolutions that are from the Spirit of God. While preparing for my second message a week later, I sat in fear and trembling at the kitchen table seeking God's word for the little congregation who would gather. Frankly, I was afraid of the reaction of many of the older Christians who would not approve of another "Spirit-filled" church in the community, and who might perceive it as competition and detrimental to the other churches already there. Apparently, I was desirous of men's approval rather than just resting in God's. Then thoughts of self-doubt and wave after wave of fear splashed over me. Was this God's leading? Was it His timing? Was I really doing this for God, or was it for my own gratification? Was I doing it out of spite, or rejection, or perhaps some kind of need for retaliation?

I began to examine my heart and cry out to the Lord for His help. Desperate to know the truth about myself, I prayed as David had, for God to search me deep within. My heart longed for assurance and a peace that would wash the doubts and condemnation away, and I cried out to God, "Lord, if this church planting idea is really my own and not Yours, I have to know it! If there is any truth to these thoughts, if they are really from You and not from the enemy, if I am acting out of presumption and selfish ambition, then show me; and I will shut this down before I do more damage to Your Kingdom and my family."

I was sitting, praying in my spirit for some time in the quiet, when suddenly, I heard someone behind me clearly speak these words, "For such a time as this I have called you!" My head snapped around to see who had spoken, but I saw no one. The words were still hanging in the air when I heard them again; this time I was aware that they were not from human lips. As God is my witness, to this day, I believe they were audibly spoken; not only did my spirit hear them, but my natural ears registered them also. I sat shaken to the bone. I had heard that others had had similar experiences, but I somehow doubted that I could ever be among them. I knew that the prophet Samuel had heard an audible voice from God when he was called; but was my spiritual hearing so dull that I needed to be shook to the bone with a more blatant experience? I felt like the proverbial donkey that the farmer had to smack with a two-by-four between the eyes just to get his attention. I think it was my own fears and doubts that God needed to address and eliminate before those shortcomings discouraged any believers and seekers who were to join us in the church. I needed to know beyond a shadow of a doubt that this was God's purpose and calling in order to be able to impart the same confidence and sense of direction to others!

After hearing these words, I searched the Scripture to find confirmation and discovered the context in the Book of Esther. My fears vanished, my spirit rejoiced, and knowing the significance of the passage and having a solid assurance of my calling, I preached my next message on January 11th. It was a call to lay one's own ambitions down and seek first the Kingdom of God. Naturally it was titled, "For Such a Time as This!"

Three days later, I began driving two hours one way to attend my first day of training at the Word of Life Church Planting School in Red Deer, Alberta. In the first class while I sat waiting for the teacher to come in to start, I silently cried out to God for more confirmation in my spirit, that I was doing what He was directing me to do. I was so afraid of missing His timing and direction more than anything else, and I desperately wanted His blessing. I had given up driving truck full-time and in faith hired a part-time driver to drive my truck, hoping that it would still provide enough finances to support my family.

A few minutes later, Pastor Mel Mullen came in and opened the class with his teaching on "Getting a Vision From God for Your Community." Remarkably, he proceeded to preach to the class the exact message I had preached to the little group who had gathered on January 4th, just nine days before. He used the same Scriptures, the same format, headings, content, and all. For 20 minutes, I sat with tears streaming down my face as I followed my own message notes, which I had left in the front of the binder that I had brought to this class. It was as though he was using them for his own class outline. I was so totally blown away by the grace of God to send such a confirmation to me. If that was not enough, God also did something later that day that was so out of the ordinary from my past experience, yet would soon no longer be foreign in my life.

"FOR SUCH A TIME AS THIS"

While we were eating our bag lunches in our classroom, a gentleman with a warm smile paused in the doorway and looked in to see who was in the room. He had realized that this was the church planting class and came in to introduce himself as the pastor of one of the Word of Life churches. He shook hands with us and expressed his pleasure to meet each of us. Later, following the day's lessons, I anxiously waited in line to speak with Pastor

Gary Carter to tell him about the lesson Pastor Mel had taught, confirming God's direction in my life. From a short distance away, I noticed the pastor from my lunch-hour introduction looking at me with an interesting expression on his face. He then motioned for me to join him and proceeded to explain his interest in me.

I'll never forget the content of his message for me, although the precise wording has escaped me. His words went something very close to this: "Pardon me for intruding on your time, but I received a vision from the Lord just now when I was looking at you. It also appeared directly over your head when I looked into your classroom at lunchtime. I feel that the Lord is impressing on me to share this with you now, and you will likely understand it better than I do. What I saw was a large wooden "Job Box" covered in dust. It was open, and I could see it was full of many construction tools used on larger commercial construction sites that were also dust laden and covered in cobwebs. Are you familiar with the kind of "Job Box" I am telling you about?"

"Of course, I am," I replied. "I have several months of experience working in the construction industry on commercial sites as a carpenter!"

"Good. Then you will understand why the Lord is showing me this picture and what it means." He went on to explain, "You are that 'Job Box,' and you are full of many tools that God has equipped you with. These tools are gifts, knowledge, experiences, truths from God's Word, and a strong desire to work in God's Kingdom in the ministry. The Lord is telling me you have been accumulating these tools to do the work of the Kingdom for some time now. Many times over the years, you have cried out to Him, asking, 'How long, Lord, before I can use all these wonderful tools and truths You have shown me to build Your Church? How long, Lord? How long?' He is answering your heart's cry today, and He wants you to know this: 'I have called you and appointed you for such a time as this! Now is the time to work!'"

He then went on to share what God was showing him at that moment. "I see an eagle on the ground with wings spread out at his sides. It's struggling to fly, but it cannot because a network of strong cords binds it down; each cord is tethered to stakes on its ends. [Immediately, a picture of Gulliver in *Gulliver's Travels* came to my mind.] I see a pair of shears coming and cutting these cords, one at a time so that the wings are free to take the eagle up to great heights. You are that eagle. You are like Gideon. You are a mighty warrior who has been tethered, unable to fly, crying out, 'How long, Lord? How long until I am free to fly?'"

I sobbed as he spoke. A more accurate picture could not have been given to explain what I had felt and experienced for more than 15 years of my life. What a joy flooded over me as he described what God wanted to do in my life and had already begun, and it struck me deeply that he had used the exact same terminology that God had spoken to me in the kitchen just a few days earlier.

About six or seven weeks later, nearing the completion of the course, the leaders of the church and school were praying for me in what is commonly known as the presbytery. On the platform with the local pastors and church leaders was Rev. Mel Davis who prophesied and gave the word of the Lord to me for this season of my life, using that same terminology while accurately describing what God was doing in my life and preparing me for in the future. God is so good; He always confirms His word to us through the mouths of two or three witnesses.

WALKING IN AUTHORITY WITH CLEAN HANDS AND A PURE HEART

And so I plunged forward with confidence into the great adventure of building a church for the glory of God. There was no longer doubt in my heart as I moved ahead week by week, teaching and preparing the church for God's purposes and establishing it in our city. But I was soon to discover that the kingdom of this world does not appreciate encountering the Kingdom of God advancing into more of what it thinks is its territory. Unfortunately, satan's cohorts have never encountered the "Borg" and are slow learners of their "motto" that "resistance is futile." It's also quite possible that they have had free reign in many areas because the Church has either been too lazy or just plain ignorant concerning the vital role it has been called to play in dispossessing these squatters from the communities or regions for which the Church is responsible to win for the Kingdom of God.

What I've discovered is that satan's little demon warriors are very good at setting up camp in the land that Christ has already won for us at the cross. However, they are mere squatters who need to be evicted by the servants of the true Landowner. Psalm 24 contains these truths:

> *The earth is the Lord's, and the fulness thereof.... Who shall ascend into the hill of the Lord? or who shall stand in His holy place? He that hath clean hands, and a pure heart; who hath not lifted up his soul unto vanity, nor sworn deceitfully. He shall receive the blessing from the Lord, and righteousness from the God of his salvation (Psalm 24:1-5 KJV).*

The earth belongs to our Father, and we have been made stewards of it. In this passage, the "hill of the Lord" is terminology often used interchangeably with "the mountain of the Lord." Both of these terms refer to a spiritual and/or governmental structure of authority. We have been promoted to a place of authority in the spiritual realm through the work of Christ at the cross. But not everyone who has been given a new spirit through Christ is walking in this authority. These verses give us a window of revelation as to why so many fail to see that authority evidenced in their prayer life or public life.

Verse 3 asks, "Who shall ascend or be promoted into the hill of the Lord?" In other words, "Who shall exercise and have authority in the spiritual government on this earth?" Verse 4 answers the question: "He who has clean hands and a pure heart, who has not lifted up his soul unto vanity, nor sworn deceitfully." This speaks of two areas of our being. The term "clean hands" is reference to our deeds or actions, what we do with our bodies. Therefore, our deeds must first be righteous and not sinful, and even our good deeds must be from a pure motive or pure heart.

Secondly, the soul must also be cleansed and holy. Our spirits might belong to God, but often we reserve part of our souls. Our soul is the battleground that the Spirit of God seeks to inhabit and control completely, while our old nature (flesh) and satan battle to dominate it. So in verse 4, the psalmist also makes it clear that our souls (mind, will, and emotions) are to be made subject to purity. Pride, rebellion, lust, anger, unforgiveness, or any evil desire should not dominate or control our inner man. We have to take responsibility for our inner man's health.

In First Thessalonians chapter 5, Paul provides a quick checklist we can use to guard our attitudes and inner man. In addition, it's very significant that Paul concludes his exhortation with the thought that our (whole) entire being is to be sanctified ("through and through"—see 1 Thess. 5:23 NIV), and he is careful to draw our attention to all three parts of our human being—the body, soul, and spirit! How important it is that we be grateful for, acknowledge, and not resist God's work in our lives even when our circumstances are not palatable!

Rejoice always, pray without ceasing, and give thanks in all circumstances; for this is the will of God in

115

Christ Jesus for you. Do not quench the Spirit. Do not despise the words of prophets, but test everything; hold fast to what is good; abstain from every form of evil. May the God of peace Himself sanctify you entirely [through and through]; *and may your* [whole] *spirit and soul and body be kept sound and blameless at the coming of our Lord Jesus Christ. The one who calls you is faithful, and He will do this* (1 Thessalonians 5:16-24 NRSV).

No authority in the spirit realm will be given unless we first take responsibility for the welfare of our own spirit. This means being good stewards of our heart's condition. Matthew 25:14-28 gives a clear picture of how the Kingdom of God's authority structure works. It is a simple principle. We are given stewardship over as much as we have ability to faithfully handle. If we are faithful in taking care of nurturing our soul with His Word and watering it with the presence of His Spirit, there will come to us a reward of greater levels of authority in the spirit realm and in the natural world.

A CONTINUOUS AND PERSONAL BATTLE

We all experience a battle in our souls daily. If it's not sparked by the images on TV, it's ignited by the neighbor's new 4x4. Or for the ladies, it might be admiring that new dress in the shop window. It might also be the cruel words spoken by a trusted friend or spouse. We get hurt, harbor unforgiveness that turns to bitterness, and before we know it, the heavens have closed. God seems so distant, and we lose desire for fellowship with Him and His family. In our homes, we men are given authority and stewardship over our children and our wives whom the Word teaches we are to love as deeply as our own selves (see Eph. 5:25-31). So, when we hold anger, resentment, bitterness, envy, or jealousy towards them, we are only setting up the home for destruction. Jesus Himself said that a home divided against itself cannot stand (see Luke 11:17). Ephesians chapter 4 identifies the gateway that the enemy uses to access our lives, with destructive attacks against the home.

> *So put away all falsehood and "tell your neighbor* [or your spouse] *the truth" because we belong to each other. And "don't sin by letting anger gain control over you." Don't let the sun go down while you are still angry,* **for anger gives a mighty foothold to the devil.** *If you are a thief, stop stealing. Begin using your hands for honest work, and then give generously to others in need. Don't use foul or abusive language. Let everything you say be good and helpful, so that your words will be an encouragement to those who hear them. And do not bring sorrow to God's Holy Spirit by the way you live. Remember, He is the one who has identified you as His own, guaranteeing that you will be saved on the day of redemption.* **Get rid of all bitterness, rage, anger, harsh words, and slander, as well as all types of malicious behavior. Instead, be kind to each other, tenderhearted, forgiving one another, just as God through Christ has forgiven you** *(Ephesians 4:25-32).*

It is these kinds of attitudes and behaviors that get imbedded into our souls and become stumbling blocks to us and others. At the same time, they also become the building blocks or materials of strongholds that keep us from victory. Therefore, we are instructed to "get rid of them all." If we do not, before long it is we who begin to believe that "resistance is futile"; hence, we give up even trying to find the source of our failures. We choose rather to blame others or the church. But the truth is, we have been ignorant of the devices and schemes the enemy has been using to keep us from taking possession of the territory that was awarded to Christ by the Father at Calvary. When we neglect to deal with these stumbling blocks, we ignore taking responsibility for our soul's condition.

So who shall exercise authority in the spiritual realms on this earth? Those people who have won the battles first in their personal lives. I'm convinced that a very large percentage of spiritual battles within our communities begins with the personal battles we face as spiritual leaders. We as pastors and church leaders will win no corporate battles in the community beyond the nature of those we've faced and won in our own personal lives. Our spiritual authority and supremacy comes from having faced and won the tests against the same demonic strongholds that control or possess dominion in our regions.

For example, let us suppose our region is controlled by the pursuit of wealth and possessions (a spirit of mammon). Before we can effectively displace that ruling spirit and witness a change in the spiritual climate in our community, we must first have faced and won dominion over the same pursuits in our own lives. This could be displayed in many ways, the first and greatest evidence being that we are faithful stewards in tithing and giving of our own increase. This giving must be in faith and to the proper recipient. For a pastor, this would not be his own church, but to those who are in authority over him personally, who speak into his life, who hold him accountable, and who also feed him and sustain him when he is going through the difficult times in his own life—in short, tithing faithfully to his own personal pastor or mentor from his personal income. His church would also need to tithe faithfully to the governing body to which it is held accountable and follow the same principles of stewardship as he is in his own life.

There might be other battles or tests that help define the arena in which satan has been able to win his supremacy over a community or region. There likely will be more than a few battles to face in a leader's life, one of which will likely be sexual purity or lust (one of satan's most successful strategies). Or it might involve true honesty, integrity, or anger issues. It might be a battle with pride and building God's Kingdom versus building our own kingdom. For more information regarding the principle of dominion in the spiritual realm and walking in spiritual freedom and supremacy, which can impact a community to the degree we have witnessed in Drayton Valley, see Pastor Gary Carter's book, *Power to Effect Change.*

The personal changes that I have witnessed, not only in my own life, but in many of my brothers and sisters, come not only from assaulting the strongholds of local powers ruling the region but from dealing with the strongholds that are in our own souls (they are often one and the same). The battles we face inwardly are often good indicators of the greater forces working in our community, but not exclusively. We might be dealing with personal areas that predate our moving into a particular community, so they can involve other strongholds also. Our battles can also indicate the nature of the spirits that have held ground in us from an early age and to which we have either been blind out of ignorance, or to which we have been made subject to by our own refusal to exercise our God-given authority. They are often the areas of our greatest weakness, perhaps because we're convinced it's impossible to win the battle, or because we're afraid to give up the comforting effect these spirits can have when we leave them alone. In this case, they can be referred to as familiar spirits, because we've become so familiar with their presence in us that we perceive them as just an attitude or personality flaw. This perception is a strong indication we are dealing with spiritual forces.

WHEN I AM WEAK, HE IS STRONG

Throughout the Bible and especially in the Old Testament, in many cases, the term "spirit" may be substituted with "attitude." (See First Samuel chapters 17-24 and the story of Saul's inner battle with attitudes, fears, and a spirit of anger and jealousy toward David and his fame after killing Goliath.) It is in our outward attitudes that we manifest our inner spirit. That is why Jesus said that *"out of the abundance of the heart the mouth speaks"* (Matt. 12:34b NKJV). These areas of weakness are the very issues that God often chooses to turn into strengths within us. We cannot take any glory away from God when we see His victory in an area we have known for years was our greatest weakness. God delights in setting His people free and in using a manner which cannot be misconstrued or misunderstood as being "the arm of flesh." God will not allow His glory to be robbed from Him! So, He chooses to use man in the area of his greatest weakness and humility.

Not long after starting a new church in our community, I attended a Red Deer Word of Life ICIN conference. One of the keynote speakers taught on Second Corinthians:

> *For though we live in the world, we do not wage war as the world does. The weapons we fight with are not the weapons of the world. On the contrary, they have divine power to demolish strongholds. We demolish arguments and every pretension that sets itself up against the knowledge of God, and we take captive every thought to make it obedient to Christ* (2 Corinthians 10:3-5 NIV).

The definition he gave for the term "stronghold" found in this passage has since helped to open my eyes regarding how to deal with the attitudes that tried to set in during the "dark ages" of my life. (Those are the times we feel abandoned, confused, lonely, or filled with despair because of the circumstances we are in; but more about that later.) His definition for "stronghold" was: "A mind-set impregnated with hopelessness that causes us to accept as unchangeable, situations that are contrary to the will of God."

This Scripture has been an integral part of experiencing the victories I've seen in my life over the last four years. I have learned how to tear down the strongholds in my life that were preventing my family and me from walking in the blessing and prosperity that is God's hope and prayer for us: *"Beloved, I wish above all things that thou mayest prosper and be in health, even as thy soul prospereth"* (3 John 1:2 KJV).

I had accepted many subtle lies about myself, my life, and areas that directly affected my marriage. Following the dream I had about my past shame and regrets, there was a season of significant change in the way I saw and understood myself. However, my wife had finally come to the place in her life where she truly believed I would never change the way I treated her or that we would experience God's blessings in our home. There was still a stronghold in her; and later, I discovered several in my own soul. These became open doorways for the enemy's assault on our home. Over a period of just a few short months, we were hit with the three highest causes for divorce. First, my wife's sister died very unexpectedly at just 50 years of age; second, financial crisis hit us; and third was our 18-year-old son's impending departure from home, following his graduation from high school. The end result—she believed that the way to save her sanity was by leaving me and seeking comfort in the friendship of another man.

Through God's sovereign work of a spirit of forgiveness and repentance, our relationships and circumstances have been steadily changing for both of us. Although much of the work was done after it was too late for marriage reconciliation, God continues to mold and mend the lives of those who have been wounded and broken by the ravaging effects of our divorce. I would like to be able to say that the fallout of my marriage breakdown was confined to my children and close family, but that is just not true. You see, because I was the pastor of a young growing church when our lives blew apart, it also deeply affected our friends and the members of the little church.

While many struggled to understand, others stood by us in prayer; and still others began to quickly condemn and align themselves on one side of the issue or the other. It left some of our newer converts disillusioned, and a number of the older Christians we had once fellowshipped with disgusted. Divorce is insidious; it not only splits up families, but it also separates and destroys their mutual friendships. It always leaves behind a trail of wounded hearts, bitter souls, and battered families. No wonder God hates divorce.

THE DESTRUCTION OF ANGER, JEALOUSY, AND UNFORGIVENESS

So the enemy used my own blindness and weakness to try to thwart God's purposes in our community and in our home. Because I refused to recognize the hand of God in the people who came to warn me of the issues I was packing in my heart that were evident to them, I had to endure the process of refining fire that was a lot more painful and drastic. But through the difficulties and trials that followed, I can now see how God directed, protected, and resurrected His hopes and dreams that once lay shattered at my feet. I will deal more with this in depth in Chapter 9, "The Job Experience." However, to apply this concept of personal strongholds and what I have learned through my own experience about them, I want to briefly share a few points.

In order for satan to develop a stronghold within us from which he can launch his attacks or thwart God's perfect will for our lives, he first must establish a foothold. With a foothold in place, he keeps working that weak area until he gets entrenched into our lives securely. Anger, envy, and jealousy are his favorite ways to enter in because with these he will often bring physical death and destruction to lives. Unforgiveness, judging others, and self-defense are three of the more common doors he uses to destroy homes and churches. Paul warned the Ephesians about anger's potential trap.

Be ye angry, and sin not (Ephesians 4:26a KJV).

And "don't sin by letting anger control you." Don't let the sun go down while you are still angry, for anger gives a foothold to the devil (Ephesians 4:26-27).

Anger in and of itself is not a sin, for he clearly says, "Be angry," but follows with, "and sin not" and instructs us to not let the sun go down while we're still angry. There is a place for anger when it is used to motivate good and right actions. Christ Himself displayed the wide range of all human emotions, and anger was definitely one we see when He cleansed the temple. It must have been quite a display, for here was a golden opportunity for the priests and scribes along with the leaders who were already plotting to kill Him to have seized Him. Yet instead of being captured, He alone cleared the money changers and livestock merchants from the Gentiles' porch (the place the public could come to seek and approach God) in the temple without help from His disciples. Anger becomes an issue or a foothold when it is inappropriate and destructive to another's physical or emotional well-being. When it is bottled up and turned inward, it can become a time bomb that eats away at your soul, destroying your ability to build healthy relationships with others. Before long, this foothold advances into the final stages of a stronghold from which satan's demons lay hidden and protected while destroying our lives. It is the core motivation for murder, and God deals with both as the same sin. (See Jesus' teachings on the Ten Commandments in Matthew 5:21-22.)

Satan established his first foothold in Cain's jealousy, which turned to anger, then murder, with the result of banishment from the family structure. Satan also sought to find a foothold in Christ after He was baptized by John the Baptist and again in the Garden of Gethsemane. Shortly before He led His disciples to pray there with Him, Christ taught the disciples at the supper table for the last time before going to the cross.

> *I will not speak with you much longer, for the prince of this world* [satan] *is coming. He has no hold* [nothing, no foothold, accusation or legal charge he can make stick] *on Me* (John 14:30 NIV).

I believe the enemy seeks to find a weakness in each of us, whether it be harboring resentment, refusing to forgive, unresolved issues of anger, or judgments against others. These are a few of his favorite, although not exclusive, traps that he tries to snare us with.

Jesus made a very strong case about harboring unforgiveness and the way we can imprison ourselves by refusing to forgive others (see Matt. 18:21-35). When we refuse to extend forgiveness, unforgiveness not only imprisons us, but it also imprisons the one we hold it against. It then keeps us from receiving the forgiveness of our heavenly Father, which we need daily. Furthermore, this unforgiveness not only opens the doors wide to the enemy and allows him to wreak havoc in our marriages, homes, financial security, and health of our own bodies, but also in our spouse and children's lives. It is important to note that when the creditors seized the debtor's property, it not only included the money and wealth he had, but it included putting him, his wife, and his children into the hands of the tormentors. I cannot honestly say that I know anyone personally who would willfully and knowingly put their own children in harm's way, yet when we consider the condition of the Church Body today, it is obvious that many are experiencing just such a situation in their families and homes.

Paul, during his discourse on the Lord's supper, also made a point of warning the Church against the prison of unforgiveness and how devastating it is to us.

> *For anyone who eats and drinks without recognizing the body of the Lord eats and drinks judgment on himself. That is why many among you are weak and sick* [not walking in divine health], *and a number of you have fallen asleep* [died prematurely] (1 Corinthians 11:29-30 NIV).

The terminology used here, *"without recognizing the body of the Lord"* is a reference to His claim in verse 18 that there was division and strife in their midst, so much so that they would deliberately prevent their brother or sister whom they were at odds with from enjoying the finer, choice dishes that they had brought to the Sunday fellowship dinner. Their resentment motivated them to heap up their plates and not leave the good food for those at the end of the line. By doing so, they were oblivious to the fact that they were hurting their own spiritual body, the Body of Christ, the church of which they were a part. This selfish, unforgiving, resentful, and bitter behavior was giving the enemy an access into the church, which was ultimately defeating their own ministry. So powerfully damaging was this behavior and attitude that the result was many were open to satanic attacks on their physical bodies to the point some were even dying. Paul called this judgment a disciplining from the Lord.

I look at it from a parenting perspective. If your child falls into rebellion and refuses to heed your warnings of the dangers involved in their disobedience, there comes a time when you've no other choice but to leave them to suffer the consequences of their actions. It's one of the most difficult situations a parent has to face, while their teenager exercises their wings of independence. It hurts you deeply to see them afterwards in painful remorse, but you know that there was no other way but to let them learn from the "school of hard knocks."

CHANGING A NATION ONE PERSON AT A TIME

The same principles that apply to the family setting, apply to us as a nation. Why is it that the Church has an incredible shortage of funds to help the poor in our communities and abroad? Why do we see such a dramatic rise in the divorce rate of Christian homes? This has not always been so! Why can't the Church turn the tide of moral corruption in the political arenas across our land? Why hasn't the Church risen to the challenge of taking responsibility for the decay of marriages and stood against the present push for the gay community to have their "unions" recognized as "marriage" in the courts? Where will this slippery slope of apathy lead this country to ultimately? We need to take action quickly, and the action must start in each of our own souls if we are to have the authority to impact the forces of darkness that battle for the souls of our children and the destiny of our nation. If we are to impact a nation, it has to change one person at a time!

Consider the list of following principles built upon one another.

1. The world influence, power, and security of a nation are determined by the strength and solidity (unity) of the society within it.

2. In turn, the strength and solidity (unity) of society are determined by healthy relationships and security within the home.

3. Those healthy relationships and security within the home are built on the moral fabric and integrity of the leadership within the family.

4. The moral fabric and integrity of the leadership within the family is molded and influenced by those whom that leader has admired, listened to, and respected throughout life.

5. Everyone gives someone they admire the right to speak into their lives and influence their moral choices and ultimately the direction of their lives.

6. The right to speak into someone's life, including our own children's lives, is earned and built through a loving and caring relationship.

7. Our children will be the leaders, movers, and shakers who mold the destiny of our nation for all future generations.

But we must remember...the power of life and death is in the tongue (see Prov. 18:21).

Loving and caring relationships are destroyed by words of criticism, judgment, accusation, fear, doubt, mistrust, jealousy, envy, bitterness, dishonesty, and malice. With our words we build up or destroy one another, and by our words we can ultimately change the course or the future of our nation. Will you be the one who begins to mold your national future and the leaders of tomorrow with words of divine purpose, power, and praise?

It's an awesome responsibility, and every day we make decisions that influence the inner character of our children and ultimately the welfare and strength of our nation. We can no longer sit back and expect our nation to automatically run itself and revert back into righteous and God-fearing practices—not in any area, be it politically, morally, financially, or educationally. It is time for us to take responsibility for our own world and to become the good stewards we were called to be. And I sincerely believe that as we take responsibility, God will restore the authority and favor His Church was intended to have, just as He instructed Adam and Eve to have in the beginning. Someone once said, "All it takes for a country to be defeated from within, is for a few good men to do nothing!" The second law of thermodynamics assures us that without a regular and committed effort on the part of righteous men (the Church) to hold a country to the reigns of righteousness, it will soon deteriorate until it is in moral chaos and decay.

ENDNOTE

1. Mel Tari, *Like a Mighty Wind* (Carol Stream, IL: Creation House, 1971), 86-87.

CHAPTER 8

Fed From the Heart

For out of the abundance of the heart the mouth speaks. A good man out of the good treasure of his heart brings forth good things, and an evil man out of the evil treasure brings forth evil things (Matthew 12:34b-35 NKJV).

The little boy wandered into the living room where his mommy sat in a rocking chair in front of the fireplace, breast-feeding his new baby sister. Having a little sister was a brand-new experience for him, for she had arrived home from the hospital only the day before. "Mommy, whacha doin'?" he asked. "Feeding your little sister," she replied. He toddled around to the front of the chair, and as he watched, his little blue eyes grew wider by the moment. Then he exclaimed with amazement, "Mommy, you're feeding her from your heart!"

FOOD FOR OUR CHILDREN'S HEARTS

As I recall this story and the words my son blurted out that day at only four years of age, I am amazed at the depth of truth they contain. I have shared it many times while preaching, to illustrate the importance of hiding God's Word in our hearts so that at the opportune moment we will have it to draw strength from. His Word sustains us, inoculates us from evil, strengthens us, prospers our soul, and brings spiritual growth, just as surely as the nutrition found in a mother's milk brings growth, sustenance, and strength to a little child. Not only is the child's body nourished by the milk, but the natural antibodies found in the mother's breast milk strengthen and fortify a baby's immune system during the early stages of development until his own little body is able to develop an effective defense system.

Along with the spiritual application, this little picture also illustrates that from the reservoir of memories, emotions, attitudes, and beliefs that are stored within each of our souls, we literally feed the little souls of our children, whether they be good or bad things. Many of these thoughts and emotions were planted there by our own parents and teachers, or those who were a part of our formative years as a child.

The Book of Luke records the teaching of Christ:

A good person produces good deeds from a good heart, and an evil person produces evil deeds from an evil heart. Whatever is in your heart determines what you say (Luke 6:45).

When you also consider His words found in Matthew 13:16-23, where He explains that the soil in the parable of the sower is parallel to the heart condition of men, we must recognize that much of how we respond to the difficult situations that come our way in life is directly related to what has been sown into our hearts in prior years. I am convinced that the critical years in life are the formative years from conception to six or seven years old, yet many people are also directly influenced by adverse events that happen for several years after that.

WHAT'S IN A NAME?

Shortly after birth or even while yet in the womb, every child receives a name. That name plays a dynamic role in determining the character and nature of that child. Often it is, in a sense, a prophetic statement of who that child will become. In my experience working with children as a support worker and in the social services field, I have learned that if the child has a loving and well adjusted home life, has at least average looks, average intelligence, and average physical stature, he or she will likely fare well, provided they have been given a name that is popular among their peers and not totally unfashionable.

I feel confident in saying from my own experience and the testimonies of others, that children with an unusual or unfashionable name in the elementary school system will receive ridicule, cutting nicknames, and scorn from their peers, even though they have everything else going in their favor. The damage to their self-esteem and ability to cope with life can be incredible and immeasurable. However, when that same child has someone who constantly reinforces their sense of worth, their value, and how much they are loved, the child will respond with a sense of confidence and handle the ridicule in a manner that soon diffuses and/or deters the ongoing abuse from continuing. The impact that the ridicule or name-calling, bullying, or abuse from outside the home will have is greatly reduced. Yet although its impact is reduced, it is not always eradicated completely. At different occassions during daily life there often comes a stimulus that triggers an inappropriate or destructive response that might or might not be accompanied with a flashback memory of the event where the pain is still hidden. In my own situation, I was not aware of the latent memory until I prayed and asked God to reveal it to me.

MASKED MEMORIES

While I was working as a support worker with a young man who had Down's syndrome, I had an experience that made me aware of how powerful a hidden memory can be. While getting to know him in the early stages of our relationship, he said some harsh and cruel words. The circumstances that led to it were simple, and I should have been prepared for the resistance I encountered. It is not in the nature of people with Down's syndrome to easily handle changes in their daily routine. So when I tried to convince him to join me in recreational activities outside his apartment in the evening rather than watching TV most of the time, he resisted my efforts and became angry. One evening as I was attempting to get him to go outside with me, he blurted out, "Get out of my life. You weren't invited here!"

Immediately I felt a sharp sting as if someone had thrust a knife into my chest. I wanted to run, and I felt my own emotions welling up inside. I fought back the angry retaliatory words that leapt into my mind, bit my tongue, and told myself that he didn't really understand my intentions. Later as I was leaving in my vehicle, I prayed to the Lord and asked Him why those words had stung so badly. My reaction was silly and unwarranted, because I knew that his words were not really a personal attack on me; and it disturbed me that his words could hurt me given the fact I already knew the nature of my client and that resistance was expected.

The Lord immediately gave me a flashback memory of an incident that occurred when I arrived at a birthday party as a boy of six. I realized there was a connection but didn't understand it. It had been a silly incident that came from a simple misunderstanding almost 40 years ago. Surely it was all covered under the blood, and I had forgiven and forgotten it...hadn't I?

The very next day while attending the "Healing Prayer" class at the Word of Life Intern School, I listened as the teacher dealt with the topic of how God heals the wounds of our childhood as we allow Him to reveal the sources of our inordinate feelings and reactions to present stimuli. Suddenly, as our teacher was talking, I understood that the connection between the two incidences was a root of rejection that was sown at six or seven years of age.

When I was in grade one or two, a fellow student was getting ready to celebrate his birthday. His mom had told him he was going to have a birthday party and that he could invite several friends over on a Friday afternoon following school. It was still a week or more away, but he was already planning who he would invite and telling us about it in the coatroom. Several of the boys were gathered around as he described his birthday plans. He pointed to many of them one by one saying, "And you're invited, and you're invited, and you're invited." I had never been to a big birthday party, and it sounded like a lot of fun. He had invited me over to his home to play after school on a couple of occasions before, and I was excited and pleased as he also pointed toward me and said those coveted words, "And you're invited!" I was so happy and eager to tell my mom about the party coming up at the end of the week. We would have to buy a gift and a card, and I could hardly wait for the big event.

When the day of the party arrived and school finally ended, I raced home to change and pick up my little gift for him. Then I walked to the store where his family operated their little grocery business and climbed the back stairs where they lived above the store. I knocked and waited until his mom opened the door and looked down at my eager face. She stood there smiling as her son came running to the door to see who had arrived.

Looking out from behind her, he noticed that it was me and then looked up at his mom and exclaimed with disgust, "Mom, I never invited him!" Needless to say, I stood there baffled, confused, hurt, and feeling rather foolish. He was quickly and quietly scolded for being rude, and I was escorted in to join the others and the party. Unfortunately, I was not really a welcomed guest, and the other boys had their own way of letting me know it. I sensed their rejection and continued to feel the sting of ridicule that followed for a time at school.

As I grew up, the details and impact of the incident were forgotten until that one day just a few years ago while in class at the Word of Life Intern Training program when I was given understanding by the Holy Spirit. I can recall growing up, experiencing many occasions where I was made the outsider and felt not welcome. In many ways satan reinforced that bitter root of rejection, from being chosen last when picking sports teams, to the kids calling me names and feigning "passing my fleas with disgust around the classroom" after accidentally touching me.

HEALED THROUGH A LISTENING PRAYER

Several weeks later, I attended a quiet and private time of "listening prayer" (also known as "healing prayer") with the teacher and an accompanying gentleman who recorded the conversation and prayer. During the private prayer session that evening, we dealt with that particular incident as well as many other childhood experiences that were revealed by the Lord in visions and through the Lord speaking to me. Consequently, a great healing took place as I forgave and released those involved in hurting me.

One of the most significant things that occurred, which came as a great shock and surprise, was the revelation that as a child of three and a half I had been sexually abused by a trusted woman who looked after me in her home. This occurred while my dad was building her new home on the property beside the home in which she was living. The Lord gave me a vision while I was sitting and quietly praying with the counsellor and while notes were being taken of all that was said during the meeting. It has since helped me understand why my marriage failed and how satan was able to wreak havoc on our home even while so many powerful prayer warriors interceded on our behalf.

Jesus was standing before me. He was dressed is the softest and most beautiful white clothing of His time while on earth. He appeared before me with one hand reaching down and looked at me with compassion-filled eyes. He did not say much, but I understood He wanted to lead me somewhere. I was only three and a half or perhaps four years old. My oldest sister was with me, and I was standing, trying to hide in the folds of her dress. I peeked out at Christ from my place of safety, and I felt His love and strong desire to touch me; but I was also aware that I was afraid to go with Him. Instinctively, I knew that the place He wanted to show me held confusion, fear, and pain. Yet how could I know this when I did not know where it was He wanted to take me?

I did not want to face the truth of what I might learn so I took my attention from the vision. I sat in the office weeping, so afraid, yet deeply longing to not grieve the Spirit of God or Christ as He was trying to help me. My counsellor asked me what I was afraid of. I couldn't give her an answer; I only knew it was a painful place that Jesus wanted me to visit. She asked me if I trusted Christ and if I knew how much He loved me. Then she prayed that the Lord would assure me that He would always stay beside me in the journey.

I grew calm, and once again as I closed my eyes, I found myself as a little boy with Jesus. I felt my sister give me a gentle push toward Jesus and heard her reassuring me that it would be all right. Then Jesus reached down and took my hand, and we walked together down a sidewalk on a street. We hadn't gone far when I found that we were standing in front of a little house with a broken-down, half-opened gate and a white picket fence in need of paint. The gate had to be lifted in order to swing it out of the way, and we walked together up the uneven cement walk that was cracked, broken, and lifting in several places. At a glance, the home appeared to be a small, rectangular, 600 to 700 square-foot bungalow. It had small covered steps and a landing that led to a screened door in the center. There was a window on each side of the door.

We walked up the steps and tapped on the door. It was opened by a heavyset older lady in a flowered dress and a dirty pinafore. I was led inside to an old mow-hair covered couch on the left and invited to sit down. She then went into the little kitchen in the back half of the house to remove her pinafore (apron). Across from me in the small living room was the door to a bedroom. I knew I did not like that place, and I did not want to be left here. I was no longer aware of the presence of Christ; only a fear and loneliness gripped me.

The lady returned with some pictures and a 3D picture viewer. She then showed me how it worked. By putting the card with two identical side-by-side pictures into the clips at the end of the arm, lifting it to your eyes and looking into the viewer, the two pictures merged into one. The picture had depth and made you feel like you were looking into a different world where life was black and white with shades of grey.

After doing this for a bit, she asked me to come with her into the bedroom. I did not want to go in there, and so I pulled my hand away from hers. She took my hand again and held it firmly in her chubby rough fingers. She then led me to the bedroom where she asked me to show her how much I liked her by doing things for her that were disgusting and distasteful to my immature and innocent mind even then. When I tried to resist and run, she locked the door and threatened not to feed me ever again if I didn't indulge her. She warned me that it must be our secret, and if I shared it with anyone else, terrible things would happen to me all my life. I vowed in my mind to bury the memories away down deep and pretend it never happened.

Because she looked after me every day and I was afraid of going hungry, I complied and tried to please her. She wanted to be kissed and touched in places I knew were not right. How I dreaded that part of my day. Afterward when she made lunch for me, I would be sure to eat as much as was allowed lest she again ask me to do those ugly things and refuse to feed me. If I could eat enough, then I could refuse her requests that she made in her bedroom, knowing I would be going home later in the day when my sisters returned from school and I could eat then.

While the details of my vision were slowly being revealed with great difficulty and pain, the counsellor would continually ask for the Lord to show me in the vision where He was and reveal the truth as to what the devil was trying to do. She would ask for the lies to be revealed and for God's love and forgiveness to hold me as I went through it. I prayed for God to forgive the woman involved, and refuted and denounced the lies about myself and about God that the enemy had sown into my tender psyche. Through the process I was never coached by the counsellor to see anything, never heard her suggest that any events happened, nor was I subjected to any form of hypnosis. It was a divine work of the Holy Spirit and a powerful revelation that corrected and set me free from buried memories and events that held me captive for years. One of the greatest lies that was uncovered was believing that as long as I could give my wife sexual pleasure, I would always be loved and my marriage would be secure. The other lie was that I would not have enough to eat or that God my heavenly Father might not have enough to take care of me. There was also a trust issue, because my parents had unknowingly sent me to a place where I was being hurt, and as a child I could not understand why they would do this.

The listening prayer event left me emotionally drained but feeling lighthearted and relieved. It seemed so surreal that I even questioned myself and wondered if I had somehow manufactured the vision in my own imagination. For several days afterward, the enemy tried to get me to dismiss its validity. He would tell me that I had imagined the whole thing in order to have an excuse for my own weaknesses and failures. Finally, I phoned my oldest sister and talked to her about it. She felt that there was a strong possibility that it was a real event, and although her memory was shadowy of a place that fit that description, she said that it was God's answer to her prayers for each of her younger brothers and sisters. I feel it was significant that it was my oldest sister in my vision, who presented me to the Lord. The Lord had already taken her through similar types of visions and healed her of childhood memories and things that were threatening to destroy her marriage. Since then the Lord had given her and her husband such freedom and healing that she exclaimed, "It's like a honeymoon we never had!"

Many weeks later, I shared the experience with another of my sisters. She cried as she also related the time frame, names, and places where the events had to have occurred. She remembered the house and was the one who knew the circumstances of Dad working for the lady. I have always had memories of seeing my father building a home in the community where it occurred. I was grateful that her memory recall ability was incredible and she could confirm that it had been a real and significant healing experience for me. While she was not aware of any harmful activity going on years before, she related having memories of a dirty feeling (sense of perversion) whenever she was in the home. She also recalled that the woman's husband had been left impotent from his sinful activities during the Second World War. I'm not sure how she learned this information, but she was old enough to have understood what it meant when she likely overheard the discussion among adults.

It is a documented and supported fact now in most of our learning institutions, school systems, and in our family and social service organizations that the painful abusive experiences (including harmful words that are spoken) that are committed against children in this stage of life often become the seeds of thought that later in life develop into the strongholds of rejection, self-loathing, loneliness, guilt, shame, or any other host of damaging emotions and thought patterns. The end result of these false images of ourselves, or false beliefs about our situations, is the creation of a sense of worthlessness, hopelessness, and despair that often leads to tragic and self-destructive behavioral patterns.

A BROKEN HEART, A BROKEN BODY—A HEALTHY HEART, A HEALTHY BODY

During his time, Solomon gathered knowledge and wisdom from sages across the earth, but his greatest source was the wisdom God had given to him as he observed mankind's behaviors. His collection of truths found in the Book of Proverbs includes many passages dealing with relationships. Take note of the following statements.

A wholesome tongue is a tree of life, but perverseness [deceit] in it breaks the spirit (Proverbs 15:4 NKJV).

Pleasant words are like a honeycomb, sweetness to the soul and health to the bones (Proverbs 16:24 NKJV).

A merry heart does good, like medicine, but a broken spirit dries the bones (Proverbs 17:22 NKJV).

His observation that a broken heart or spirit will cause physical problems and affect a man's whole well-being is now supported by physicians worldwide, and there has been a rapid rise in the acceptance and practice of wholistic medicine in the western world. We are finally realizing the impact that our words have on others in our lives. And while we can bring healing and restoration by asking those we've wounded for forgiveness, very often the experiences that damaged us as children can only be effectively and expediently dealt with by the work of the Holy Spirit and our heavenly Father who sees the very deepest part of our souls.

Doctors today tell us that the only time the body can truly heal itself after an injury or during a sickness is while we are resting. Consequently, they prescribe rest for us when we are sick. Likewise, we need deliverance and rest from painful emotional wounds that we received throughout our lives as children and during the developing years as teenagers. If our body's well-being is hidden in the marrow of our bones, it only makes sense that the author of Hebrews understood the impact that the work of Christ and the Word of God would have in bringing healing to the wounded soul. When it comes to issues of the soul, we need the rest that only Christ can give us through the cross in order to be healed.

> *There remaineth therefore a rest to the people of God. For he that is entered into His rest, he also hath ceased from his own works, as God did from His. Let us labour therefore to enter into that rest, lest any man fall after the same example of unbelief. For the word of God is quick, and powerful, and sharper than any twoedged sword, piercing even to the dividing asunder of soul and spirit, and of the joints and marrow, and is a discerner of the thoughts and intents of the heart. Neither is there any creature that is not manifest in His sight: but all things are naked and opened unto the eyes of Him with whom we have to do* (Hebrews 4:9-13 KJV).

As I read these words, I find a beautiful description of the work of God as a surgeon of the spiritual man, and I see myself in the operating room having been put to sleep under the aesthetic of the Holy Spirit while God operates with His Word to remove the damage and foreign objects of guilt, shame, and regret imbedded in the inner man. This all was made possible because Jesus Christ paid the hospital bill for me in advance at the cross.

Luke 4:16-19 records that Jesus said He came to fulfill the prophet's words found in Isaiah 61:

> *The Spirit of the Lord God is upon Me; because the Lord hath anointed Me to preach good tidings unto the meek; He hath sent Me to bind up the brokenhearted, to proclaim liberty to the captives, and the opening of the prison to them that are bound; to proclaim the acceptable year of the Lord* (Isaiah 61:1-2a KJV).

These are the prisons and chains of our own making. Jesus came to break those prison doors open, snap off the chains, cancel the power of these lies, heal the damage of the abuses suffered, and eliminate the impact of the lack of nurturing from a parent during our critical years as a child.

In the previous chapter, I used the illustration from the teachings of Christ found in the "sower and seed" parable. I explained that the "stones" or "adverse soil conditions" that Jesus referred to are the hidden conditions of the heart, which the enemy of our souls uses and capitalizes on to ensnare us and to rob from us the blessings we should be enjoying. Some of the sources for these "hidden stones" are the words children hear spoken over them or silent messages we give them by our actions. These can be words that parents speak to their children; the comments or careless remarks cast over young sensitive hearts by elders, relatives, or teachers in elementary school or Sunday school; or the constant ridicule of siblings at home or peers at school. Then there is sexual abuse and physical abuse, which can include ongoing neglect and absence of food, proper clothing, comfort, security, praise, or words of love and affirmation; not being included in meaningful and uplifting conversation at home between children and parents or older siblings; constantly being ignored or shut down when wanting to say something; or simply not being included in games, parties, and fun times most children experience as they grow up. The presence of any or all of these negative factors can determine the way a person is able to cope with everything life dumps on their doorstep in later years. These factors can directly impact the level of a person's success and the frequency of his failures.

While some have endured an existence that included many of these factors and then overcame them by sheer willpower, many others continue to be held captive by the negative factors and consequently suffer silently for years. But we know for certain that when given words of positive affirmation, a secure home, and a strong awareness of being loved by parents and by God, a child's odds of overcoming life's obstacles increase dramatically. Even if it is later in their childhood or teenage years when they are given these foundations for successful living, they can still discover that God is at work in their lives helping them to turn repeated failures into eventual success. Thus, they have the power to become better not bitter when the painful experiences and chapters of life unfold.

WORDS THAT LOVE AND WORDS THAT KILL

By our words, we speak life into our children; and by our words, we can also condemn them and speak death. Indeed, how often have we spoken and declared lies over our children, lies that satan wants them to believe about themselves. We can break their tender spirits with words like, "Why do you *always* have to be so clumsy?" "Can't you *ever* get anything right?" "You never pick up after yourself!" "You *lazy bum*, get off your butt and help clean the house!" "You *stupid* little…!" And the list goes on.

I recently saw an advertisement on TV sponsored by a society that works to eliminate abuse towards women, which illustrated this same point. A young lady behind a fast-food counter is wearing a name tag that reads, "Filthy Little Whore"; another salesclerk's tag reads, "Fat Ugly Bitch"; still another receptionist's, "Slut"; and the nameplate on one gal's office desk, "Lazy No Good Bum." Then the screen goes black and the following words appear while they are spoken: "If they hear it often enough, they soon begin to believe it! Verbal abuse is still abuse!" It is a powerful message and is greatly needed.

Still, the question is, where did men learn to treat their loved ones like that? No doubt from parents at home as they were growing up. When a person hears words enough times, he or she soon begins to believe them. Why do we speak cruel, harsh words in absolute terms that are lies spawned by the deceiver himself? How many times have you overheard some angry young parent lose their patience and tear apart their child until that child bursts into tears of anguish? Have you ever been pricked in your heart with a sense of injustice or experienced a wave of remorse for your own lack of control sometimes? We should be!

> *A man's stomach shall be satisfied from the fruit of his mouth; from the produce of his lips he shall be filled. Death and life are in the power of the tongue, and those who love it will eat its fruit* (Proverbs 18:20-21 NKJV).

These Scriptures clearly indicate that our words are powerful enough to destroy a person's spirit and are like seeds that when scattered in soil eventually bring a crop of fruit. We literally fill our lives and our children's lives with good fruit or evil fruit, life or death, blessing or cursing. Our tongues are powerful beyond measure, and learning to guard and control them is a difficult task indeed.

> *If people never said anything wrong, they would be perfect and able to control their entire selves, too. When we put bits into the mouths of horses to make them obey us, we can control their whole bodies. Also, a ship is very big, and it is pushed by strong winds. But a very small rudder controls that big ship, making it go wherever the pilot wants. It is the same with the tongue. It is a small part of the body, but it brags about great things. A big forest fire can be started with only a little flame. And the tongue is like a fire. It is a whole world of evil among the parts of our bodies. The tongue spreads its evil through the whole body. The tongue is set on fire by hell, and it starts a fire that influences all of life. People can tame every kind of wild animal, bird, reptile, and fish, and they have tamed them, but no one can tame the tongue. It is wild and evil and full of deadly poison. We use our tongues to praise our Lord and Father, but then we curse people, whom God made like Himself. Praises and curses come from the same mouth! My brothers and sisters, this should not happen....But if you are selfish and have bitter jealousy in your hearts, do not brag. Your bragging is a lie that hides the truth. That kind of "wisdom" does not come from God but from the world. It is not spiritual; it is from the devil. Where jealousy and selfishness are, there will be confusion and every kind of evil. But the wisdom that comes from God is first of all pure, then peaceful, gentle, and easy to please* (James 3:2b-10,14-17a NCV).

This passage declares the power of the tongue and compares the tongue to two things—the rudder of a ship and fire. The tongue is only a small part of the body, but it has the power to determine the course of life. It can lead us into destruction, or into blessings. It can set the course for others' lives also, especially our children.

We are to have a spring of life flowing from our mouths which brings blessing and life to everyone around us (see verses 10-11). Furthermore, our words must sow peace in order to raise a harvest of righteousness (see verse 18). Yet how often do we leave our children's deeply impressionable minds in anguish and turmoil because we have torn them apart with destructive words, or an unappeasable attitude? If they never receive a sense of satisfaction by pleasing their earthly parents, they will not likely be able to sense the pleasure that God feels when they are loving Him and serving His purposes in this life.

As parents we would also do well to pay great attention to Paul's words to the parents in the church at Ephesus.

> *Fathers, do not **exasperate** your children; instead, bring them up in the training and instruction of the Lord* (Ephesians 6:4 NIV).

The word "exasperate" speaks of having frustration to the point of anger, hopelessness, and giving up the task as unobtainable. In other words, because there has been such a high standard of expectation set, a child feels it is impossible to attain. Then without getting a sense that parents are pleased with their efforts, they quickly grow frustrated and angry, and in hopelessness they give up trying to do the right thing altogether.

It is important that our attitudes and words don't communicate disdain and disappointment, but rather love, acceptance, encouragement, and a sense of pride in their attempts to please and do what's right. Verses 9 and 10 in James chapter 3 clearly state that if our mouths are praising and blessing God, they should also be as quick to praise and bless our children (made in God's image), rather than curse them and find fault with everything they do that we don't like.

THE GIFT OF APPRECIATION
AND THE PAIN OF INGRATITUDE

Not only can we damage our children's fragile souls over a period of time, but we can also destroy our spouse's soul by failing to build them up, strengthen their inner man, or encourage them and appreciate their attempts to display their love for us. Knowing their love language and how they express their feelings of love is a key to appreciating them in our lives.

The importance of words and their impact on loved ones is a hard lesson I learned. The following story comes to mind, dealing with the topic of "feeding from the heart" and the "overflow of words" that can build or destroy those we love the most in our lives. It took place during the separation period and prior to the divorce of my first marriage.

I had moved out of our home to give my wife some space and an opportunity to consider our future together while we received counselling. However, after several months, she filed the divorce papers. Under financial pressure, she also insisted that we put our house on the market for sale. I reluctantly agreed and renewed my efforts to prepare the home to sell. We painted and cleaned, sorted and sold as much stuff as we could. It was a painful experience and one that certainly dashed my hopes. I would work on the outside and in the garage, while she painted the bedrooms and halls—we seldom worked together as it was too distressing for her.

One evening I dropped in to pick up some tools I had left behind and found her painting the doors and trim in the hallway. I offered to help, but she was almost finished. We got into a conversation about where our lives were headed, and the words were filled with pain and regrets but still remained kind and non-accusing. Not far into the conversation, her pager went off. She was on call as the fire department's dispatch operator and had to respond immediately by rushing over to the fire hall to handle the emergency. I assured her I would stay behind, finish the project, and clean up the painting equipment before leaving.

When I finished painting the door inside our bedroom, I set the brush down and sat on the bed to inspect the finished product. I was a perfectionist to some degree and was critiquing the work in my own mind. I looked around me at the now bare walls which were also being prepared to be painted before the house went on the market. I noticed that the wall where a picture had once hung had a faint hue of the older color coming through, and immediately a flashback memory hit me from several years earlier.

Although I had promised to paint the bedroom, the cans of paint had been setting on the closet floor for weeks, while I found myself too busy with other activities. In the meantime, my wife had offered to do it herself, but I had insisted she let me do the job. Then one day (five or six weeks later), I arrived home to find the bedroom furniture stacked in the middle of the room and my wife standing, looking "proud as punk" (where did that saying come from?) with a paint roller in her hand, rose-colored paint in her hair and on her chin, and a smile on her face, having just put the finishing touches to her masterpiece. Without considering all the hard work she had done, I immediately berated her for not waiting for my help. You see, I was a bit of a perfectionist (did I tell you that already?), and her painting expertise had never measured up to my standards. I didn't express any gratitude, and to make matters worse, I also proceeded to point out the places where the paint had not covered the old color properly, or she had touched the roof with the roller. (I was a real jerk to say the least!) She burst into tears, and I stood shocked at her emotional outburst. Eventually, later that night after suffering from cold-shoulder syndrome and hard-couch dreams, I saw the real value of her efforts and reluctantly apologized.

Now, as I sat there, the events of that day scrolled through my mind and I thought to myself, *You big jerk. Do you see now where your ingratitude and insensitivity has gotten you?* I looked up at the discolored wall again, and it became almost invisible in the light from the bulb overhead. The thoughts had lasted only 30 seconds at most. As I sat in silence with tears of regret streaming down my face, the Lord spoke to me as clearly as a church bell on a cold winter's night. His words were not hard and cruel but cut me to the very core as I realized the magnitude of their truth. "Ernie," He said, "do you realize that she could not physically see those imperfections that your eyes were blessed to be able to see? She needed eyeglasses, but time after time she would put off an eye appointment to make sure there was enough money for the other things your home needed."

I was overwhelmed with remorse and repentance. The realization was like being hit in the stomach with the end of a bat. I sobbed as I remembered many other times when I had grumbled and criticized rather than expressed true appreciation and gratitude. The underlying attitude of ungratefulness for what God had blessed me with had been a major contributing factor in her feelings of inadequacy and inability to please me. She had given up, and I had exasperated her to the point of hopelessness for the marriage. Although I related this to her the next day, it was not enough to change the direction she was headed.

Thank God He is the God of second chances and He can change us so that our attitudes don't need to keep us wandering in the wilderness for 40 years like the Israelites who grumbled and complained rather than appreciated the daily blessings and miracles their God was giving them. Our own pride and insensitivity blinds us to the wonderful gifts God gives us. If it is not our pride, then our fears and lack of faith and trust in God prevent us from truly walking into the land of promise and purpose God has prepared for us to possess. But once we see our own ignorance and heart condition, and repent and turn back in true remorse, God is faithful to cancel the impact our sin should have had on our lives and sets things right, in order for us to receive His best again.

CHAPTER 9

The "Job Experience"

After Job had prayed for his friends, the Lord gave him success again. The Lord gave Job twice as much as he had owned before (Job 42:10 NCV).

It was late on a December evening, and I sat on the edge of my bed in quiet retrospect. I was deep in thought concerning where my life had finally ended up. At this point, I was 40 years old and in the middle of divorce proceedings. I had two wonderful children—a 17-year-old son who struggled to speak to me because of the anger he felt over the whole situation and a 14-year-old daughter who bravely faced each day with hope for a better future for both of us. She also had difficulty making sense of it all and constantly fought within herself to remain impartial. I was filled with remorse and regrets, which the Lord was clearly dealing with in me.

151

His Word was daily becoming more alive and personal. We held long conversations, and the comfort He gave me was always enough to see me through each day. He understood the pain and the purpose for it all, and this became my hope. At that time, the desktop screen on my computer showed a picture of two deer standing in the middle of a broad stream in the mountains. Around them, the mountain sides blazed with a raging forest fire while they stood calmly drinking from the cool waters. I had overlayed the picture with several Scriptures from the Psalms, which served as a healing reminder of God's promise to maintain control and work in my life.

> *He leadeth me beside still waters. He restoreth my soul. As the deer pants for the waters, so my soul longs after Thee. For though I walk through the valley of the shadow of death, I will fear no calamity for You are with me* (Psalms 23 and 42, author's paraphrase).

Every day, along with my daily prayers, I would say a prayer that God had given me a year before as part of my devotional time. It had poured forth from the Scriptures in almost the same order that I give you here today. Without a doubt, it brought a solid confidence that God was indeed still in control of my life and His purposes would ultimately reign supreme over my own fears and regrets. Following are the words I prayed on that night in December for the umpteenth time!

MY PRAYER FOR GOD'S PURPOSE IN MY LIFE

We know that all things work together for the good of them who love You, Lord, to them who are called according to Your purpose (Romans 8:28).

And though I walk in the midst of troubles, You will strengthen me. You shall stretch forth Your hand against the attack of my enemies, and Your right hand will rescue and protect me. For You, O Lord, will accomplish perfectly that which concerns me. Your mercy, O Lord, endureth forever. You do not forsake your handiwork (Psalm 138:7-8).

I am confident of this very thing, that You who began a good work in me, will continue to work out Your purposes in me until the day of Jesus Christ (Philippians 1:6).

Therefore, I trust in You with all my heart, and I lean not on my own understanding; in all my ways I acknowledge You, and You shall direct my paths in life (Proverbs 3:5-6).

I gain understanding from Your precepts, and therefore, I hate every wrong path (Psalm 119:104).

You declare, O Lord, that the thoughts, plans, and purposes You have toward me are thoughts of peace and not evil, to give me a future and a hope (Jeremiah 29:11).

For Your thoughts are beyond my thoughts; Your ways are higher than my ways. So I will not lean on my own wisdom and knowledge, but trust in You alone (Isaiah 55:9; Proverbs 3:5).

*I will entertain **no fear** of sudden disaster or of the ruin that overtakes the wicked, for You, Lord, are my confidence. You will keep my foot from being snared and from stumbling, for You guard the way of Your faithful ones* (Proverbs 3:26; 2:8).

Your promise is that the steps, plans, and affairs of a good man are determined and ordained, ordered and directed by You, Lord; and I can delight in Your plans for me (Psalm 37:23).

Your word is a lamp to my feet and a light to my path (Psalm 119:105).

Because You have saved me and called me with a holy calling, not determined by my works, but because of Your own purpose and grace, which was given to me in Christ Jesus even before this world began! (2 Timothy 1:9)

This holy calling and the gifts You put within me are without repentance. You will not remove them, and they will make a way for me (Romans 11:29; Proverbs 18:16).

I rejoice, for You, Lord, are able to do exceedingly abundantly above all that I ask or imagine, according to Your power that is at work within me (Ephesians 3:20).

You, Lord, grant to me, according to the riches of Your glory, to be strengthened with might by the Holy Spirit in my inner man, that I be filled to the fullest capacity so that I might accomplish all that You have called, appointed, and planned for me to do in this life (Ephesians 3:16,19; Psalm 37:23).

Lord, I pray this in order that I may live worthy of You and may please You in every way—bearing fruit in every good work, growing in the knowledge of God, being strengthened with all power to Your glorious might so that I may have great endurance and patience. That I might joyfully give thanks to You, Father, who has qualified me to share in the inheritance of the saints in the Kingdom of light. And that I might stand before You, Father, and hear You say, "Well done, good and faithful servant. You have been faithful over a few things; I will make you ruler over many things. Come and enter into the rest I have prepared for you and share in your Master's happiness!" (Colossians 1:10-13; Matthew 25:21)

(*All Scriptures above are author's paraphrase.)

THE PROMISE OF BLESSINGS

After praying these words, I sensed His presence in the room with me just as I had sensed His presence on the first day He had given the Scriptures to me. I opened my Bible to the Book of Job where I had found myself on many evenings before. As I read the last chapter, my eyes were transfixed on verses 10, 11, and 12.

After Job had prayed for his friends, the Lord gave him success again. The Lord gave Job twice as much as he had owned before. Job's brothers and sisters came to his house, along with everyone who had known him before, and they all ate with him there. They comforted him and made him feel better about the trouble the Lord had brought on him, and each one gave Job a piece of silver and a gold ring. The Lord blessed the last part of Job's life even more than the first part (Job 42:10-12a NCV).

Previously, I had found myself identifying with Job's laments many times, but today I was reading about the outcome of all he had been through. After suffering the shame and desertion of his wife, friends, and much of his family, the Lord blessed him and returned to him a double portion of all he had lost. Deep in my heart, I felt the Spirit of God speaking to me: "Your restoration will be like that of Job's. Wait on Me, seek My face, do not turn to the right or the left, but hold fast to the promises I have given you and the words that My servants have prophesied over you." He also gave me the passage in Joel 2:

I will pay you back for those years of trouble. Then you will have plenty to eat and be full. You will praise the name of the Lord your God, who has done miracles for you (Joel 2:25b-26a NCV).

To confirm this Word, He immediately led me to Second Chronicles 20:20. This is a Word for every Christian who wants to have clear and perfect vision for his or her life. I call it the 20/20 promise.

> *Have faith in the Lord your God and you will be upheld* [sustained in the battle]; *Have faith in His prophets and you will be successful* (2 Chronicles 20:20b NIV).

Wow! The secret to success lies in our holding fast to the faithfulness of God to perform His promises and the willingness to listen to His prophets when their word comes from God's throne. I recalled the many times my heart had burned with the excitement of hearing God's Word expounded to me and how His servants would pray over me. The same message was always reiterated: "Your life is His. You will speak to many nations. Your heart is for God's people! God has a special plan to use you to touch many people around the world. You will be going into difficult places, but do not fear; I am with you and will give you success and victory!"

How these things were to come about was not clear to me then and still remain in the shadows of the future; but what really became imbedded in my spirit was the words that "The Lord gave Job twice as much" as he had lost.

This restoration process began as I purposed in my heart to forgive and pray for my wife's friend. I had expressed forgiveness at the moment I had learned the truth about the extent of their friendship, but later had struggled to keep my heart free of bitterness and anger. There were days I felt like slashing the tires on his van when it was parked out front of her place. I had spoken some very direct and hurtful words to him early in the situation. But I prayed through the feelings and held on to the hope of a change of heart for many, many months. What I realized later was that even though Job's restoration had come, it did not begin until *"After Job had prayed for his friends"* (Job 42:10a). Through continued prayer and asking God to bless rather than punish, my heart's feelings lined up with the head knowledge that I should walk in forgiveness rather than bitterness. I was eventually able to obey God and stop to speak with this man and ask for forgiveness for things I had said in anger, as well as extend forgiveness to him. I began to take ownership of my own failures and ceased to put all the blame on the two of them.

It was only one day after speaking to him that my son sat before me asking me to forgive him for things he had said and felt toward me early on in the whole ordeal. Since that moment, my relationship with my son has been restored, and I have come to understand the power of forgiveness in binding and loosing those whom our attitudes affect. I had given my son the freedom to come to me to express himself because I had finally obeyed God and removed the stumbling block I had become to him.

Job had to express a repentant heart for his attitude and ignorance also, before he was to see God reverse the situation for him. We need to get to the place where we can acknowledge and repent of our faults, failures, and iniquities. This can involve any of the following: releasing past painful memories and forgiving those involved, identifying and being set free from generational curses, and correcting our faulty belief systems. Sometimes we need to do a checkup from the neck up and correct some "*stinkin' thinkin'*," as my office manager used to say when I worked for Met Life. Then when we ask God for restoration, He can freely and completely restore us back into His divine purpose for our lives.

THE RESTORATION OF JOB

First, Job acknowledged that God was still in control.

Then Job answered the Lord: "I know that You can do all things and that no plan of Yours can be ruined" (Job 42:1-2 NCV).

Second, he realized that God's ways are beyond our understanding; that he was saying things that were not truth, and God wanted him to learn this; and the things that were happening in his life were still ultimately serving God's divine purpose!

> *You* [the Lord] *asked, "Who is this that **made My purpose unclear** by **saying things that are not true**?" Surely **I spoke of things I did not understand;** I talked of things too wonderful for me to know. You* [Lord] *said, "Listen now, and I will speak. I will ask you questions, and you must answer Me"* (Job 42:3-4 NCV).

Third, he confessed that at one time he thought he understood God's purposes and ways, and knew Him; but in reality he only knew *about* God. But now, while he still did not understand God's ways, he knew God personally! He had gained *spiritual enlightenment* or a *personal revelation* of God's character and person. This is far more than head knowledge that leads to a belief system; it is heart knowledge which leads to faith and trust at a much deeper level.

> *My ears had heard of You before, but now my eyes have seen You* (Job 42:5 NCV).

He could see God through a different set of eyes, and from a deeper revelation of the person and Father nature of God. The difference is like studying about a celebrity's likes, dislikes, where they live, and the style of clothes they wear. Yet having never met or spent time with them, can you say you really know them? Knowing someone is to be a close friend or family member who spends time with that one. Job had discovered the difference, and the experience had brought to the surface some hidden misconceptions and deep fears that allowed the enemy the right to ask for permission to test Job's motives for serving God.

The test was simply to see if Job was serving God for what God would give him and bless him with, or serving God because of God's wonderful nature, character, and who God was. While satan wanted to drive Job into despair and away from God, God knew it would only serve to strengthen Job's resolve to serve such a wonderful Creator who loved him and was in control of his life. God was really dealing with Job's belief system, not his moral conduct. In the end, Job's motives were proven righteous and his hidden fears put to rest (see also Job 3:25). He came away from the experience a stronger, more confident, deeper trusting, and greater loving servant and child of God! Where once he saw himself as a servant of the Most High God, now he understood he was a son of God. Where once he feared God and avoided evil out of respect for God's power and wrath (see Job1:1, 28:28), now he loved God and served God out of an awareness of God's love for him!

Fourth, he repented for his self-righteous attitude and his fears. He said,

So now I hate myself; I will change my heart and life. I will sit in the dust and ashes (Job 42:6 NCV).

Proverbs says, *"For as he* [a man] *thinketh in his heart, so is he"* (Prov. 23:7 KJV). Paul taught us to "put on" the mind of Christ (see Eph. 4:23-24), which we have been given according to First Corinthians 2:16; and as we allow His mind to control our actions, we are transformed and our lives changed (see Rom. 12:2). It took a conscious choice on Job's part to change the perception he had of God. He repented for his wrong attitudes and thoughts; then he chose to adopt a new perspective of God as well as a new understanding of how God viewed him. He came to understand that God viewed him as a son, not a servant, and was pleased with him enough to brag on him to satan. He saw his own true worth before God.

Fifth, he prayed for his friends. He asked God to bless them and to forgive them of their folly also. This was not easy, considering the things they had said as they sat in judgment of him. Their philosophy was not sound; nor was their assumption that Job had committed some kind of transgression true, or that he had broken a moral law that deserved God's hand of punishment. God was not punishing Job but preparing Job for a higher level of responsibility and blessing. He had been a good steward and would now be an even better steward.

We are not to judge others based on the difficulties they are experiencing in their lives. Only God knows the reasons we face what we face. Many people sympathized with my own dilemma for a season; then slowly many of my friends began to drop away. (I was not an attractive personality to be around all the time). In time, I learned about true friendships. My true friends neither blamed Cindy nor judged me for the marriage failure. While they never agreed with the course of action that came, they tried to understand and be there when we needed someone to listen or to lean on. They offered kind advice and stood with me in prayer, believing God for the best. They took me into their home for Thanksgiving or Christmas dinner along with my daughter to help lessen the impact at those especially difficult times. If I was clinging to the hope of reunion, they also agreed with my prayer. When I finally chose to honor her choice and let go of her, they also stood by me then. They also encouraged her while speaking the truth in love and helped her through the ordeal as best as they could even when they could not justify or understand her choices. These are true friends.

In the story of Job, it's also significant that Elihu was the only one of the comforters who came to Job, who God never disagreed with or cast a judgment against. As you study his words, you find he simply kept pointing to God's divine nature and righteous character. He was simply saying, "Don't get angry at God, Job. God knows what He's doing in your life. Learn from this and trust Him!"

Sixth, he got on with his life. He was willing to start over, to love again. The account is not completely clear as to whether he was reunited with his first wife or took a new wife in the course of time (I suspect the latter), but what is important is that *he did love again* and had a second family. His new life was blessed, and he prospered so much (twice as much livestock and six times the oxen) that there was enough wealth to be able to pass an inheritance on to his sons as well as his daughters.

I've had many people express their support for me as I went through difficult times, and again later, they also shared their happiness at how God continued to bless my life. The restoration has been so powerful and complete that recently when my first mother-in-law was on her deathbed, she called to have me come for a visit. She asked for forgiveness for her lack of support in our marriage at a time when we both needed it. She requested I oversee her funeral and preach the Gospel to her family and friends, many of whom did not know the Lord. The reception two weeks later at the funeral was overwhelming as many outstretched arms welcomed my new wife and me at the funeral home. Their gratitude and response to the word that God had given me was also very uplifting as I realized how faithful God is to His word in our lives. I'm convinced that because I was obedient and not ruled by emotions but rather conquered them with the power of prayer, forgiveness, and His anointing, I opened the doorway for receiving a blessing and miracle from God. I have experienced a true "Job restoration."

TWICE AS MUCH

Today, years later, I look back at what my life has become, and my children and friends will confirm that God has truly blessed me with a double portion. He has returned everything I lost through the divorce and has blessed me with more than twice as much of everything. I now have four (not two) God-fearing, God-loving, and God-serving children. I have been blessed with a new wife who is an awesome intercessor serving the Lord in the church and community, and she's also a great supporter of my ministry regardless of where God leads us. I live in a home almost three times the size of the one I had to sell in the divorce settlement; we drive three newer loaded vehicles; and I earn a salary double what I left behind to come to Drayton Valley. I have dozens of new friends, and I've seen God use me to bring many into the Kingdom. I have been privileged to become a part of a strong church that supports and stands behind us and that is impacting areas across Canada and around the world through what God is doing here!

While the material blessings have been wonderful, it is in the realm of inner healing and ministry that God has truly been faithful to bless me; the outward blessings are merely a reflection of an inward change. I have found that I am no longer easily offended. I no longer hold on to a poverty mindset but have begun to recognize the pattern of thinking that accompanies it and to deal with it in myself when it tries to come back. I know that through Christ I am worthy to receive God's best because His gifts are not a reflection of who we are but of who He is. I do not feel rejection where none was intended. My patience level has increased dramatically. And oh, one other curious side result—I have found a new ability to stick with home projects right through to completion, even the large and distasteful ones. God continues to deal with my "soul issues," for it is in these areas of my life that I needed the touch of God the most, and because of His work I can sit today and write the words you have been reading.

KEY PRINCIPLES TO LEARN FROM THE BIBLICAL ACCOUNT OF JOB

1. Regardless of how terrible life becomes, God is still there and He still cares about you! If you are a child of

God, then God is ultimately in control of your circumstances and you need to acknowledge that fact daily. It helps you keep a proper perspective! Praise Him regardless of circumstance, then circumstance will turn into opportunity to witness God's miraculous power and to bring blessings and freedom to others. (Also see the story of Paul and Silas in prison.)

2. God will allow satan to test or try us, to prove our faith, but He will never allow us to go through more than we are able to endure! And always remember that satan has to get permission. Ultimately, we are the ones who give it, simply because of human nature's tendency to conceal things from God.

3. In order to share in the blessings of God's Kingdom, we must also be prepared to share the cup of His suffering that Christ paid for us. This suffering often comes as ridicule, judgment, ostracism, criticism, or misunderstandings that cause a breach of fellowship. It might also include (but is not limited to) physical suffering, mental anguish, or imprisonment.

4. Forgiveness releases God's hand to work in our lives in areas where we have hindered Him and His purposes. Praying for and speaking a blessing over our enemies will ultimately open the door to personal freedom and dissolve the power and ability for others to hurt us. If God asks us to forgive an indefinite number of times, it's only because we also need that kind of forgiveness extended to us.

5. We reap what we sow. If we sow forgiveness, we'll reap forgiveness. If we sow grace, we'll reap grace (and we all need more grace). If we sow blessings, we'll reap blessings. God always reserves a special blessing for us if we keep serving Him regardless of how many of our closet friends turn away from us.

6. One day we'll see things from God's perspective and His purposes will be revealed. We will truly rejoice at His awesome power and blessings. Just as we've been given a view of the activity in Heaven concerning Job's life, eventually we'll understand God's involvement and purposes in our own. But until that day, it is very important to keep an attitude of gratitude while thanking God for His involvement in our lives and praying for our friends and enemies.

7. Our God is all-powerful and always in control even when we can't understand His workings. God can always turn the situation around no matter how dark, difficult, or impossible it seems to us! God is a God of second, third, and twentieth chances (from our perspective), and He will set us back into His intended purposes and blessings once we have been through the fiery testing period and dealt with the thing(s) that caused us to stray from His will. He is never limited to only one plan to bringing about His purposes.

CHAPTER 10

The God of the Second Chance

You have allowed me to suffer much hardship, but You will restore me to life again and lift me up from the depths of the earth. You will restore me to even greater honor and comfort me once again (Psalm 71:20-21).

I was praying one day several months after writing the previous chapter and meditating on God's goodness and the nature of His character when the phrase, "He's the God of the second chance" came back to my mind. I pondered it for a moment and then thought to myself, *I really need the God of the fourth and fifth chance considering how many times I've blown it.* God spoke to my heart right then and said, "No, Ernie, I'm the God of the second chance, and that is all you'll ever need!" Now I'm not one to debate with God much anymore; I've done my share of that in the past, and it's a funny thing—I always lose those debates. But on this occasion,

I was rather intrigued by what God had said to me so I took the bait and asked Him, "God, I know that Your mercy endures forever, and there is no end to the number of times we can be forgiven, so why do we need only two chances? I don't understand, Lord."

He replied, "If you've come to Me after you've blown it and asked Me to forgive you, then I have. There's your second chance and you start over. If you blow it again and come to Me again for forgiveness, don't bother bringing up your past failures. As far as I'm concerned, they never happened; they're lost in the 'sea of forgetfulness,' and I have no record of them. Remember, I've already forgiven you; and when I forgive, I also choose to forget. So, it will always and forever only be your second chance. It's only you who keeps score and an account of how many times someone needs another chance."

Wow! He really is the God of the second chance! What confidence that gives me when I approach His throne of grace. Every day I wake up and realize, *today is my second chance to get it right.* How many second chances do I get? As many as I need to get it right! So now, I watch for patterns of failures, and then I take the necessary steps to change. To get to the root issue that's been tripping me up all along, I ask God to search my heart and know my motives in much the same way David did in Psalm 139:23.

If you're feeling like a failure and you've been down the same road so many times you're ready to quit trying, remember, you haven't failed until you've quit. Maybe you feel your history is just too filled with bad things, things you've never told anyone about because you're so ashamed of them. Then take a look at this list, which was circulated to me through an email and which I have slightly revised. It includes people in the Bible whom God chose to use. It might surprise you, but I think God excels in using failures to do His work. In fact, He favors it!

The next time you feel like God can't use you, just remember…

- ❖ Noah was a drunk.

- ❖ Abraham and Sarah were too old to be parents.

- ❖ Isaac was a daydreamer.

- ❖ Jacob was a liar.

- ❖ Leah was ugly.

- ❖ Joseph was abused.

- ❖ Moses was a murderer who had a stuttering problem.

- ❖ Gideon was afraid.

- ❖ Samson had long hair and was a womanizer.

- ❖ Rahab was a prostitute.

- ❖ Jeremiah and Timothy were too young.

- ❖ David had an affair and was a murderer.

- ❖ Elijah was suicidal.

- ❖ Isaiah preached naked.

- ❖ Jonah ran from God and was prejudiced.

- ❖ Naomi was a widow.

- ❖ Job went bankrupt.

- ❖ Peter denied Christ.

- ❖ The disciples fell asleep while praying.

- ❖ Martha worried about everything.

- ❖ Mary Magdalene was a whore.

- ❖ The Samaritan woman was divorced more than once, and sleeping with another woman's husband.

❖ Zacchaeus was too small and a unjust, thieving tax collector.

❖ Paul was a religious gang leader who had Christians murdered.

❖ Timothy had an ulcer, and...

❖ Lazarus was dead!

Now! No more excuses! God can use you to your full potential.

Besides, you aren't the message; you are simply the messenger.

Let me close this book with a story and prophecy that Cindy Jacobs shared in her recently published book, *The Voice of God*. It perfectly illustrates how our relationship with God is the safety net for all our screw-ups in life. It's not a licence to fail but a recipe for success.

> Recently it seemed our local Body (i.e., local church) was under a lot of attack and discouragement from the enemy. The Lord spoke a word of comfort to us that broke apart the despair. It went like this:

> "There is a subtle deception coming upon the Body, trying to make them feel that I do not care about their every need. It has come through trying circumstances and problems that wear My children down and make them doubt Me. For there are things that have happened to you that you cannot explain, things that have not been as you planned. But I say to you, My children, even if you have missed My voice through your own foolish plans, am I not greater than your mistakes? Can't I take these and turn them for good? For if you make a mistake and Plan A doesn't work then I have a Plan B and if Plan B falls apart I have Plan C. Haven't I said I will never leave you nor

forsake you? Is there anything in your life too big for Me to handle? For I am your provider and a good Father. I am not here to berate you for your mistakes but to give you another chance, for I am the God of the second chance. I am the Lily of the Valley, I am the cleft in the rock, I am the good Shepherd and I see the end from the beginning. There is nothing you have need of that I cannot take care of, for I am an extravagant God. So trust Me; know that I am with you. I will never leave you nor forsake you."

At the end of the prophecy, the church began to praise God. Tears streamed down many faces. The Lord had comforted Zion [His Church Body] with His word and presence and our lives were changed by His Love.[1]

If you have struggled for years to get it right and have been caught in a cycle of defeat that keeps you going in circles, ask God to show you the original violation that trapped you in the cycle in the first place. It might take some difficult soul-searching or revelation, and you will likely have to be brutally honest with yourself; but the end results and rewards are well worth it, my friend.

If you are not sure how to go about this, or are not familiar with how God speaks to reveal this to you, there are several ministries you can contact, which assist individuals who want to be set free from past bondages or childhood wounds. I recommend that you search on the Internet for *Elijah House Ministries*, or pick up any book on inner healing by the authors John and Paula Sanford. You can also order teaching materials, books, and other information regarding prayer ministry by contacting *Elijah House Ministry*'s website: elijahhouse.org.

Do not put off what God has been wanting to do in your life. If your heart was burning within as I shared my own testimony and as I spoke of the truths from God's Word, know that was the Holy Spirit convicting you and revealing the truth to you. You too can have your life changed and continue to change as my life continues to change. It really is an exciting and ongoing process—a journey with eternity's end in view. God will strike your heart with the cords of His love and bind you up in the bundle of the living. True life can be yours and you can experience living at its best. Turn your whole life over to Him today, and allow Him to do a complete work in your past, present, and future!

God bless you as you consider this offer. If you've been changed as a result of what I've shared on these pages, please email your testimony and your story to:

erniecs@telus.net.

Be sure to put in the subject line: *I was changed by your story!*

ENDNOTE

1. Cindy Jacobs, *The Voice of God* (Ventura, CA: Regal Books, 2004), 108-109.

Contact the Author

Ernest Cowper-Smith

4545 – 42 Ave
Drayton Valley, Alberta, Canada
T7A 1G6

E-mail: erniecs@telus.net

Phone: 1 (780) 514-4722 or 1 (780) 621-0200

Additional copies of this book and other book titles from DESTINY IMAGE EUROPE are available at your local bookstore.

We are adding new titles every month!

To view our complete catalog online, visit us at:
www.eurodestinyimage.com

Send a request for a catalog to:

Via Acquacorrente, 6
65123 - Pescara - ITALY
Tel. +39 085 4716623 - Fax +39 085 9431270

"Changing the world, one book at a time."

Are you an author?

Do you have a "today" God-given message?

CONTACT US

We will be happy to review your manuscript for a possible publishing:

publisher@eurodestinyimage.com